Anonymus

American Husbandry

Volume II.

Anonymus

American Husbandry
Volume II.

ISBN/EAN: 9783742837226

Manufactured in Europe, USA, Canada, Australia, Japa

Cover: Foto ©Andreas Hilbeck / pixelio.de

Manufactured and distributed by brebook publishing software (www.brebook.com)

Anonymus

American Husbandry

AMERICAN HUSBANDRY.

Containing an ACCOUNT of the

SOIL, CLIMATE,

PRODUCTION and AGRICULTURE,

OF THE

BRITISH COLONIES

IN

NORTH-AMERICA and the WEST-INDIES;

WITH

Observations on the Advantages and Disadvantages of settling in them, compared with GREAT BRITAIN and IRELAND.

BY AN AMERICAN.

IN TWO VOLUMES.

VOL. II.

LONDON,
Printed for J. BEW, in Pater-noster-Row.
MDCCLXXV.

AMERICAN HUSBANDRY.

CHAP. XXV.

GEORGIA.

Climate — Situation — Soil — Productions — Agriculture — Exports — Observations.

GEORGIA is in many respects the same country as Carolina, differing very little in climate, but generally in favour of it. Upon the coast it is not above sixty or seventy miles from north to south; but in the internal country the distance is upwards of one hundred and fifty miles. The climate upon the coast is hot, damp, and unwholesome, like Carolina, though there are hilly spots which form strong exceptions. The flat country extends in general about two hundred miles from the sea, and the interior tract, which reaches from thence to the Apalachean mountains, and is about one hundred miles broad,

broad, ranks in every respect among the very finest in all America. The climate at the same time that it is hot enough to produce the most valuable staples, is healthy and agreeable to an extraordinary degree; free from those sudden changes and violent extremes that are felt in the maritime part of the province, and which are so pernicious to health wherever found. In this country the soil is of a fertility that even exceeds the back parts of South Carolina, especially on the river Savannah, and its branches to the west and north-west of Augusta, and indeed all round that town: no flat lands are found, no swamps, no marshes, but high, dry tracts, waving in gentle hills, and the vales watered with numerous streams. The soil a deep black loam, so rich that there is scarcely any exhausting its fertility: it was for a long time unknown that such a country existed here; but upon first settling Georgia, and for many years afterwards, the flat sandy coast was the only part of the province attended to or known; and as long as this has been the case with any of our colonies to the south of New York, they have languished, and emerged from their languor as soon as they penetrated into the rich and healthy

part

part of the country. Georgia was a very inconsiderable province as long as the people confined themselves to the coast; but the efforts since made here have been by means of removing backwards, where silk, indigo, and other commodities of great value, are cultivated with a success far greater than was ever found in any of the maritime parts of our colonies. But however clear the excellencies of these interior parts of Georgia may appear, to such as have viewed them with an understanding eye, yet are they not one tenth peopled: it is but a few years since any attention at all has been given to this province by American or European settlers; but after the arrangement of the American governments in 1763 had confined all the colonies to as narrow bounds as the encroachments of the French before the war, and their operations in it, they then found good land, unpatented, scarce; which pushed them upon a more industrious search: this was the cause of Georgia receiving since the peace such an accession of people, that settled in numbers in the back parts of it; and it was the same cause that contributed to the peopling several districts in North Carolina, which had been long neglected.

The soil and face of the country in the maritime part of the province, resembles South Carolina; it consists of a flat territory, very sandy, and in general either pine barrens or swamps; the slips of oakland are not large or numerous: the swamps are inferior to those of Carolina in the production of rice, and in general the country is not so good for the whole breadth of the flat part; but this inferiority is not great; all the sea-coast of America, from Jersey to Florida, has a strong similarity.

The vegetable productions both of trees, shrubs, roots, flowers, &c. are the same as those of South Carolina; nor is there much difference in the growth, for though Georgia lies to the south of that province, yet is the climate not hotter than that of Carolina; and there are some parts of the latter, particularly Charles Town, much hotter than most in Georgia. Relative to a further account of the soil, climate and products of this province, I shall here insert an extract from a letter written by a planter, who went from England and settled not far from Augusta, and has resided there eight years.

" I must freely own, that in some instances I was much disappointed in my expectations

pectations of this country,—I thought the soil had been more generally good, and the climate I was taught to imagine was more agreeable to an English constitution; but in summer I find the heat very oppressive, and gives one, for two or three hours in the afternoon, a languor which I never experienced in England even in the hottest days; going out is then disagreeable, and the only way to be tolerably at ease, is to keep one's self perfectly quiet, to sit still in rooms that admit much air but no sun, and to be cautious in diet: this season lasts through July, August, and most of September. The way to enjoy the agreeable parts of any avocation during those months, is to rise early in the morning, and to transact whatever business requires your being abroad, by eleven o'clock, or at most by twelve (unless the days are cloudy), and then to keep the house till five in the afternoon: in the evening the air is cool enough to render the fields pleasant. What I have now told you is not general with all constitutions; I have a servant, who came from England with me, that feels no more inconvenience from being exposed through the heat of the day to the sun, than the very negroes themselves, who generally

delight

delight in the most meridian beams; and among my neighbours, I know two or three who are of the same temperament. But my own constitution is very different, for a fever would be the least consequence I believe; and indeed I partly know it from experience, which would ensue from my using any fatiguing exercise, from one to three o'clock in the afternoon in summer, when the sky is clear; for with a south wind the sun's beams are so intensely hot, that the only pleasure I feel, is to be perfectly at rest.

"But at the same time, Sir, that I describe these inconveniencies, let me remark, that I should use very different terms if I lived near the coast: I have been often at Savannah, when I have longed ardently to be at home; the climate is there beyond comparison worse than at Augusta, and the farther west we go, the better it becomes. This will doubtless appear very strange to you, as there is so little difference in the latitudes of these places; but that is a circumstance which has little to do with climate in this part of the world. I attribute the great contrast there is between the sea-coast and the western part of the province, to the flatness of one, and the varied

ried surface of the other—also to one being full of swamps and marshes, and the other being entirely free from them. Flat countries have always less wind and agitations in the air, which render it far more pure and wholesome to breathe in, as they carry off speedily every noxious quality; there is scarce an instance on the globe, of a hilly or a mountainous country being unhealthy; even under the line or the tropics such are always inhabited by a hardy and robust race of people. The other circumstance is of yet more consequence; the effluvia of stagnant waters in a hot climate, and especially of such as rice-swamps, which are shallow, sometimes fields of mud, at others thinly covered with water, cannot but prove prodigiously injurious to the health of the human body, at the same time that it renders the heat not only burning, but close and suffocating: such a thick heavy atmosphere, in a country so flat as not to be windy, must necessarily make the maritime part of this province far more hot than the internal part, creating a difference greater than what many degrees of latitude could occasion.

"In the observations have made on the climate's being uncommonly hot, I confine

fine myself entirely to the hottest part of the summer, July, August, and part of September, and perhaps, but not always, a week the latter end of June. As to the rest of the year, you have no idea in England of the charms of this climate at a distance from the sea. March, April, May, and June, are a warm spring, in which scarce a day offends you: the sky is a clear expanse, clouds rarely to be seen, and the heat nothing offensive; the beauty of our country is then enjoyed every hour of the day—in short, no season in any part of the world can hardly be more agreeable than these months in the back country of Georgia. The latter part of September and October are also perfectly agreeable, in being sufficiently warm without a melting heat. But this is not all I have to say in our favour; for to me the winter is a most pleasing season here; the degree of heat is that of a warm spring, with some days as hot as a common summer; but in some months in the latter country I have felt days as hot as are generally experienced in Jamaica: ideas of heat should not therefore be taken from the height to which the thermometer rises in certain days, but to the mean height when every day is registered.

giftered. In the winter feafon, and alfo in fpring, we have extreme cold winds, particularly the north-weft; and alfo fharp frofts; but the fudden changes from heat to cold, which are fo much complained of on the coaft, are rarely felt with us in any fuch degree as is common there. I have heard many of my neighbours complain of thefe frofts and cold winds, but to an European conftitution they are natural, and are certainly wholefome whenever the changes are not fudden from heat to cold; and even in that cafe they are better than conftant heat, if any caution is ufed in drefs. I muft fay for my own part, that neither froft nor wind have ever proved difagreeable to me; and that upon the whole, I much prefer the climate to any in which I have lived before; and yet I have refided at Cadiz, Naples, and the Weft Indies, not to fpeak of Bofton and England. But whatever I have mentioned on this head is relative only to the country to the weft of Augufta, that is, the weftern half of Georgia; for the other part does not by many degrees enjoy fo good a climate."

In another letter was written as follows. " The foil in this neighbourhood is good; in general, we have very little that is bad;
and

and none that will not produce some useful crop or other. Like you in England we have wastes uncultivated, which spread almost over the whole province; but our wastes are such only for want of people to accept their property, whereas yours are such from being of a poor and almost worthless soil. I have travelled over parts of Scotland, and even the northern counties of England, which carry such an aspect of barrenness, and are so dreary and waste, as nothing in all this country can be opposed to them. All land here that is uncultivated, is either a very rich and valuable forest, or a meadow, which in its natural state would be worth ten -- ------1--- shillings an acre in England. On the coast they have swamps, which produce nothing, tho' not many, but here swamps are rare; the low grounds on some of the rivers are more properly marshes; they are small, and such as are found in the best and most beautiful counties of England; low meadows on rivers, wherever they are found, were (in a state of nature) marshes: we have none but what might easily be drained, and would then be the richest meadows in the world, especially if kept as watered ones.

Even

Even these marshes are with us found full of tall and beautiful cedars and cypresses.

"Our flat tracts, or more properly the surface of gentle waves of country, rather than levels or hills, are of a rich loamy soil; the surface from twelve to eighteen inches deep of a fine light, black, sandy loam, which has the appearance of being the earth which has been formed by the rotting of vegetables; and yet, which is extraordinary, we have this soil where no trees are found. Under this loam we find another of a reddish brown colour, three, four, or five feet deep, and then meet with clay, and in some places rock; this under-stratum of loam has the appearance of being admirable land. Other tracts of this sort, and especially the sides of hills, are covered with a reddish loam, with many stones in it, from one to two feet deep, and under it rock: the appearance of this soil is not so good, but on experience we find it to be very fertile. In some vales, between gentle hills, we find the black loam three or four feet deep, a soil which I am persuaded might be applicable to any purpose in the world. A true clay on the surface is scarcely ever found in these tracts; but in the low lands on the river sides the

soil

soil is a very strong loam, near the clay. Some of the rivers, however, run among the hills, with high rocky shores. For 150 miles from the sea the country abounds with what they call a *pine barren*, which is a light white sand, very poor, covered with pines; it is reckoned the worst part of that country; we are not entirely without it; here and there is a pine barren, but they are rare. There are other varieties of soil, but not in considerable quantity; we have sandy tracts, which though light are very rich, and of a nature entirely different from the pine barren sand. Some spots on the rivers and the highest hills are rocky, and so rough as not to admit of culture; but these are covered with forest trees, and add very much to the beauty of the country.

" Uncultivated tracts of country in this part of America are very different from such in other parts of the world; the plenty of the finest timber is astonishing to an European upon his first arrival. We have several sorts of oak which come to a pro­digious size, twice or thrice as large as oaks in England; and some of these are much more excellent for ship-building than is commonly imagined: an injudicious choice of of the fort of oak, was for some years the cause of this idea; but later trials have diffused a more correct knowledge of the value of our timber, for some has been found superior in duration even to British oak. This wood is also cut into various articles of lumber, which are exported to the West Indies; pine, cypress, and cedar, are likewise appropriated to the same use: this is a vast advantage annexed to those parts of the country which have a good water-carriage, since these sorts of woods converted into lumber will pay the expences of clearing the thickest forests in this country, even if a proportion of the timber be of other sorts, and not used in building: when this is the case therefore, a man enters not only into the possession of an estate without expence, but even an estate that is ready to cultivate.

"Our forests are generally open, consisting of large trees, growing so thin that you may generally ride through every part of them, rarely having any underwood, and in some tracts they are wide enough for waggons to pass every where: the labour, therefore, of clearing, when the wood is not of a proper sort for lumber, is not great. We have immense numbers of wild mulberry

berry-trees, upon the leaves of which we feed our silk-worms, without forming any plantations for that purpose. Walnuts and hiccories are also very plentiful upon the best lands, and grow to a very great size."

A third letter contained the following particulars. " My plantation is situated on a small but navigable creek, which falls into the river Savannah, about thirty miles west of Augusta; when I first came, I had a very large tract of country to chuse in, for the settlements to the west of that town at any distance from it were not numerous; had I then been as well acquainted with agriculture as I am now, I could have made choice of a plantation, consisting more entirely of rich land; but as it is, I have no great reason to complain, and what I lose in soil, I gain in the extreme beauty of the situation.

My house is on the side of a hill; behind it is a fine spreading wood of oak, walnut, hiccory, &c. before it a large tract of grass which I have cleared, and which is bounded by the river, whose course I command from almost every window, for three miles on each side: on the other side of it, and all round the lands adjacent to my house, are the fields which I have in culture. The whole plantation, which is my property, confifts of 6340 acres, at leaft, in the rough manner in which the furveyor-general's people reported the furvey, that is, the quantity regiftered; the only fence which furrounded it for fome years, was trees market with a hatchet, or croffes dug in the meadows, with here and there a poft fet up; but other fettlers having fince fixed near me, who have taken up fmall grants of land, their fences have been made in fome places in my boundary line, which have faved me the trouble. In fome places I am yet open to the country not granted away; for this tract of land containing a large proportion of excellent foil, I paid not quite one hundred pounds, including every charge and fee incurred in order to procure it.

"The method here taken, is for the perfon who wants land to fix upon a fpot and take what he likes, under condition of peopling it in a given number of years: I had twenty allowed me, but they are now giving only ten or fifteen years. It is not common to fee people fixing by each other; they generally plant themfelves at a diftance, for the fake of having an uncultivated country around them for their cattle to

range

range in : all the country not granted away belongs to the king, and is common for every man to turn his cattle upon, but not in the manner such right is enjoyed in England, where the same thing is done not by permission but by right; for here every new comer has a liberty of fixing in this common part of the country, and inclosing his property immediately if he pleases; so that the lands on which we turn our cattle farther than our own bounds, are continually decreasing: the consequence is, the planters who on this account have not range enough for their large stocks, take up new grants of small quantities of land farther to the westward, for the sake of sending their cattle thither, by which means they are enabled to keep very great stocks, even so far as a thousand head. . I have four hundred and forty head of cows, oxen, bulls, heifers, &c. but their value is far from what it would be in England.

" The plenty of timber in this country is a great advantage to new settlers, in rendering their buildings and many of their utensils of no other expence than that of labour, tools, and a little iron. My house, a barn, a stable, and some other conveniencies, cost me no more at first than one hundred

dred and seventy-four pounds in cash, and the labour of ten negroes during three months; this was done by hiring carpenters, and paying them by the month; and two of the slaves learnt so much of the art in that time, that by working since with them occasionally, they are become good carpenters enough to raise a shed, or build any plain outhouse, such as you see common in England in little farm-yards: our wood is of so little value, that their making waste is of no consequence. I have made many additions to my house since, at a small expence, so that it is now a very convenient and agreeable habitation.

"When I consider that for one hundred pounds a man may in this rich and plentiful country buy an extensive tract of land; that for two more he may raise a good house and offices; that he may buy slaves for thirty or forty pounds a-piece, or hire white labour a very little dearer than in England; and that he may settle himself with as few as he pleases, and increase them as he can; when this is considered, it surprises me to think that more people of small fortunes do not come among us, but that they should prefer the narrow way in which they must live in Europe. The
plenty

plenty of this country is much greater than you can think of; a little planter, that is a good gun-man himself, or has a slave that is so, may in half a day kill much more game than two families will eat in a week; and in parts of the country where it is comparatively scarce, an easy walk will yield him a day or two's subsistence of this sort for a moderate table. By game we here understand deer, rabbits, wild kine, and wild hogs, turkies, geese, ducks, pigeons, partridges, teal, &c. Our rivers are equally abounding with excellent fish, which is an advantage not inferior to the other; and the two together in hunting, shooting, and fishing, affording a diversion equal to what is met with in any part of the world, and superior to most. Sporting here is carried on with unlimited freedom, and in a style far superior to what I have any where else met with; and whoever keeps house in this country must presently find the immense advantages attending the great plenty of these articles, which reduce all expences of this sort very low. And now I am giving you the information you want on this head, I shall add, that our great plenty of fruit is another point in which this country is very fortunate; we have melons, cucumbers, water-melons, peaches, pears, apples, plums, &c. &c. in any quantity we pleafe, almoſt without trouble or culture. The climate is fo favourable, that to plant them is all the attention requifite. Upon a new fettler fixing, one of his firſt works is to inclofe and plant a large orchard. Peaches are the moſt plentiful of any kind of fruit: a ſtone fet, becomes a bearing tree in three years, and the fruit that drops from it rifes in young trees; fo that a fingle tree would become a wood of peaches in a few years, if they were not grubbed up.

" You fee, Sir, from this account, upon the truth of which you may abfolutely relie, that you want for nothing in this country that nature can give us. Rich land is plentiful; building no where fo cheap; game, fiſh, fleſh, fowl, and fruit, in the utmoſt profufion; labour by flaves very cheap, by fervants not dear. And to this may be added a government mild and equal, in which more liberty is no where to be found; taxes too trifling to be mentioned, and where neither tythes nor poor's rates are to be found: may I not therefore conclude, that if mere living well, plentifully, and at eafe, be confidered, no country can exceed,

exceed, perhaps not equal, this. In respect of society, we are deficient; but this is made up to a studious person, or one who does not dislike retirement, by the amusements of the field, by the employments of agriculture, and by reading; not however that we are without company; I have eight or nine neighbours within twenty miles of me, with whom I visit; and some of them are families in which a rational conversation is by no means wanting!"— In a successive letter the same person gave the following particulars.

—" Respecting the agriculture we pursue, about which you enquire, I shall give you the best account I am able: the objects most attended to are Indian corn, wheat, and provisions, which long occupied this country chiefly; but for a few years past silk and indigo have made great strides among us. The country near the sea is not near so fertile in corn and provisions as that about us; we therefore not only send great quantities for the West India export, but also to feed the towns and rice plantations in part. I am much in doubt whether the common husbandry of raising corn and provisions be not as profitable as that of indigo or rice; the best planters

planters we have, and it is the same in Carolina, do not reckon they make in total product above 20l. or 25l. each for their working hands: I have exceeded this some years by Indian corn, wheat, &c. and some of my neighbours have carried it much farther than me, by more skill and closer application.

"The first business in our husbandry is clearing the ground, which is for corn, generally done by grubbing the trees up by the roots in order for the plough to go: this method I have followed in all the land I have cleared: the expence is small, from the ease of stirring the light soil; and after raising my house, offices, and negro camp, with lengths and posts for fences, &c. the residue I have sent down the river in several sorts of lumber, as boards, planks, staves, pieces, casks, &c. to Augusta and Savannah, but not with such advantage as others lower down on the river, who have not such a distance: after clearing, I have planted the land with Indian corn, for three and four years successively, and got from thirty-five to sixty bushels an acre, and at the same time from twenty-five to fifty bushels of Indian pease an acre. Of wheat my crops are not so great; but from thirty

thirty to forty bushels an acre is my usual crop. Barley we also sow, usually after wheat or Indian corn; I get the same quantity as of wheat; I have some fields, the soil of which is so rich, that I have got for six years successively crops of these kinds of grain, and all equally good, and I do not now find that the soil has much abated of its fertility; but in some of my fields, it begins to wear out; but fine grass will come, and soon yield nearly as good profit as middling crops of corn. I do not think our farmers in England grow quite so many successive crops of corn as we do here, yet I imagine our products to be much the largest. I have never laid on any dung or other manure for corn.

" My black deep loams, which were covered with wood, yield kitchen plants of very fine flavour and an extraordinary size; I allotted a piece of it near my house for a garden, in which several articles of common product much exceed what I remember seeing in England, and yet I have never manured it: this, however, is much owing to climate. I have raised cabbages of 60 lb. weight, and turneps of 25 lb. Potatoes thrive astonishingly in it; I have had 300 bushels from a bed, which in size

did

did not exceed a quarter of an acre; and several of my neighbours having found their great increase in this soil, have begun to go pretty much into them as an article of sale: they find a ready market at Savannah for the West Indies. I design taking the same hint, and believe they will be as profitable as any other article.

"There is one circumstance in this country which is very valuable in planting; it is the warmth of the climate rendering it unnecessary to house or otherwise attend cattle in winter more than in summer; they find their subsistence in the woods and natural meadows, and return home of nights only for the sake of food given them, not so much through necessity, as to induce them to be regular. Our swine fare yet better, for the woods abound greatly with mast and fruit of various sorts, which they are greedy in finding, and keep themselves fat on; but we use them to come home in the same manner as the kine. The number of hogs kept in this country by every planter is very great; they who begin only with a sow or two, in a few years are masters of fourscore, or an hundred head; I have above three hundred of all sorts and sizes, and in a few years, if the country does not settle very fast, shall have twice or thrice as many. Pork and beef barrelled make a considerable article of our product; and hides are not the most inconsiderable part of the product of our cow kine.

"Besides the articles I have mentioned, we cultivate indigo, silk, tobacco, and hemp, but not in such large quantities (silk excepted) as they do in Carolina; I have them all upon my plantations; indigo and tobacco require the same soil, which is the richest and deepest we can give them, but it must be dry; tobacco is but just coming in, but we make as good, if not better than any in Virginia; and I am of opinion, since the price has risen, it will be as beneficial as any article we can go upon. Hemp is sown in the low lands on the rivers and in drained marshes, where the soil is a stiff loam, upon clay: we do not reckon it so profitable as either indigo or tobacco; but as the land which suits it is not the right sort for those crops, it is cultivated in small quantities. I cannot speak with any precision of the products which my neighbours gain of these commodities, but I can tell you pretty accurately what I have done myself. When I had increased
my

my ten negroes to twenty, from that number, eight of whom were women (who I should observe do as much field-work as the men) they made me, with the help of five white labourers,

	L.	s.	d.
36 acres of Indian corn, the produce of which sold for in sterling money,	146	13	8
26 acres of wheat, the produce of which sold for in ditto,	93	8	0
12 acres barley, the product of which sold, yielded	18	10	0
40 barrels of pork at 1l. 12s.	64	0	0
26 ditto of beef at 1l. 2s.	28	12	0
16 acres tobacco yielded 12 hogsheads	96	0	0
33 pounds silk,	30	0	0
420 pounds of indigo from 4 acres and a half	52	10	0
Hides, live stock sold, and small articles,	47	18	0
£.	577	11	8

This product from 25 hands is above 23l. each; but the two following years I had not such good success. You see, by this account, that I made 33 pounds of silk: this is an article which deserves more attention than has been given it, either by the inhabitants of this province, or in encouragement from the mother-country: the number of hands who made this 33 lb. in a season was but eleven, which is 3 lb. a-head. This appears to be a very considerable object; among them were four of my

my children (who did it by way of amuse-
ment, and indeed a very rational one it is),
and three women; they did not employ
seven weeks in it, and I need not tell you
that in this business it is but a part of the
day that is employed. Georgia has, proportioned to its inhabitants, made a greater
progress in feeding silk-worms than any of
the other colonies, but yet her people do
not make near the quantities they might;
supposing they made but two pounds a-head,
and less than this I have never made for
every person I have employed in it, this
would be a vast acquisition for all the women, many of the children, the old men,
and disabled persons, with proper assistance
from others; and in Carolina, where the
people are so much more numerous, the
importance of the object would in a national light be still greater. This is so fa-
vourite a theme with me, that were I to
trouble you with all I could say on the subject, I should go near to exhaust your pa-
tience.

" Hemp has been too inconsiderable an
article with me to come to market, but I
hope next year to send two or three tons
down to Savannah. It may be to your satisfaction also to know, that I have made
some

some trials of wine, not yet as an export, but have used several small casks in my own family, which have proved better than I expected. Four years ago I planted about a quarter of an acre of a dry rocky spot of land, hanging on the side of a hill, to the south of which I thought promised well; I used setts of our native grapes, having no others; these are so plentiful all over the country, that you can scarce go an hundred yards without meeting with numbers. This little plantation, which, for want of better knowledge than I could gain from one or two treatises on the vineyard culture, was not managed near so well as it ought, has turned out much better than I expected. I have made wine from the same grapes growing wild, and have the satisfaction to find that the produce of my cultivated ones is beyond comparison of a finer flavour, which shews that we have much to hope from attending well to our native vines; were they managed with the skill that is exerted in the wine countries of Europe, they would perhaps turn out among the profitable articles of our husbandry. One of the neighbouring planters, a Frenchman by birth, has written to France to a relation, to send a vigneron,

well

well experienced, with some setts of the Burgundy grape: this is to be done at my expence, and I have good expectations from the scheme; though my neighbour is quite of a different opinion, and thinks that (farther than our own consumption) if I make it succeed, the culture will not prove near so profitable as indigo: how far this will prove true, I am not yet a judge. Madeira, which is the only wine we import, comes very dear to us. If we could make a sort sufficiently good to be substituted for that, it would be a great acquisition. I shall give you the account of my sale in a year since the former, being nearly what my present produce is.

	l.	s.	d.
50 acres of Indian corn, produce in sterling money	187	14	0
35 acres of wheat produce in ditto	132	0	0
20 acres of barley ditto	35	0	0
50 barrels of pork,	82	0	0
40 ditto of beef,	50	0	0
Hides,	24	10	0
Live stock sold,	30	0	0
Lumber,	36	0	0
47 pounds of silk,	47	0	0
16 acres of tobacco, 11 hogsheads,	88	0	0
Indigo,	87	10	0
£.	799	14	0

The number of negroes 25, and 5 white labourers, 30 in all; the total divided gives 26l. a-head; and this I believe may generally be equalled by those who have any luck in fixing on tolerable land, without possessing great skill in choosing the best.

"This, Sir, is a very important part of the information you request me to give, as it explains to you what is to be expected from settling in this country; I have little doubt of your friend being able to make from 20l. to 30l. a-head annual produce, sold at market, for all the working hands he employs, besides supplying the plantation with all the provisions consumed, both by the family, slaves, cattle, poultry, &c. this however is not profit; for negroes cost at present from 40l. to 50l. a-head, if good ones are bought. Cloathing, physic, attendance, &c. come to something, and distempers will now and then break out among them which prove very destructive, though in general the increase will keep up the number. Implements, tools, furniture, manufactures, &c. &c. are all much dearer than in England, except the articles which are made of wood. Wine, tea, sugar, and spices, are some of them dearer, and none of them cheaper, than in England. Re-
pairs

pairs of buildings is an article of some expnce. Negroes must have an overseer, at the annual expence of from 40l. to 60l. All these and some other articles are deductions from the planter's profit; nor should I omit to add, Sir, that the nature of the country, as it prevents many of the expences which are common in England, so it brings on us others, of which you know nothing. Hospitality, to a degree totally unknown in Europe, is the virtue of all America; and a man can hardly through inclination, but especially from example, be niggardly on any occasions that call for it; his great expence will be wine, rum, and a few other articles of house-keeping; not that this amounts to any thing very considerable.

"In general, our planters are very much on the thriving hand, yet few are rich, though I have heard of some large fortunes in Carolina; we have scarce one in the province whose circumstances do not improve. As to making a fortune, I believe no part of the world is better adapted for it, provided the planter is skilled in land, has a good degree of knowledge in matters of agriculture, and is very industrious and attentive to his business: you may easily suppose

pose that all these qualifications are necessary; indeed I know of no business in which money is to be made without knowledge and industry: I must also add, that he ought to have his capital, especially if it is not considerable, free; for interest here is 8, 9, and 10 per cent. and money even on such terms very difficult to be got; he should therefore possess, or raise whatever he wants, in England, for no dependance is to be had on getting any here.

"There are very great advantages in the husbandry which is carried on in this country, of a nature not general in others, especially in Europe; the quantity of land to be had by any person that pleases, is a circumstance no where else to be met with on the globe, at least in countries where the religious and civil liberty of mankind is secured; and among all our colonies, none has better land or a more favourable climate than the back parts of Georgia. The expences of living are low, and particularly the necessaries of life so very plentiful, that subsistence is no where easier gained; on the contrary, the articles of merchandize produced here yield a large price, as it is the nature of mankind to rate luxuries much higher than necessaries, and not to
let

let the value of one depend on that of the other. Thus the planter feeds and subsists himself and family very cheap, while he sells his produce very dear: silk, indigo, wine, hemp, tobacco, &c. are by no means necessaries, but their value is much greater: this is a circumstance of great value to the planter; how far you enjoy in the same in certain articles produced in England, I am not a good judge; luxurious articles may be very dear, but the necessaries which support the planters and their workmen are dear also."

These extracts, from pretty long correspondence carried on with a view of settling a relation in Georgia (which is since done), I am happy in being allowed to insert: it is true they principally concern only one plantation, but they abound with many valuable circumstances that concern the whole province, and as such could not but be deemed highly worthy of insertion.

The following is a state of the exports of Georgia, upon an average of three years since the peace.

	£.
18000 barrels of rice, at 40s.	36,000
Indigo, 17000 lb. at 2s.	1,700
Silk, 2500 lb. at 20s.	2,500
Carried over,	40,200

Brought forward,	£. 40,200
Deer and other skins,	17,000
Boards, staves, &c.	11,000
Tortoise-shell, drugs, cattle, &c.	6,000
	£. 74,200

But since this account was published the articles are most of them very much increased; the rice is raised to 23,000 barrels; and the price to 3l. 10s. so that this article alone makes more than the whole of the above articles; the indigo is proportionally increased, but the silk is declined: the Indian trade at Augusta is also thriven very much of late.

Before I take my leave of this province it will be proper to mention the large tract of country lately acquired by the government of the Cherokees, containing by estimation about seven millions of acres. This country lies to the westward of Augusta, and is bounded on one side by the Savannah's branches; from the description I have heard of it, I apprehend the plantation described in the above letters very nearly resembles it: the soil is as rich as any part of America; every article of spontaneous vegetation, luxuriant in the highest degree: the climate, like that of the western part of all our southern colonies which bounds upon the Apalachean mountains, as desirable as any in the world, both for the production of profitable staples and healthiness. It is further said to be as well watered with streams and rivers as can be wished, with three or four of them navigable for large canoes. Many are the people who have given in petitions for grants of land in it, so that it is expected in Georgia the whole tract, large as it is, will be settled in a few years: the articles of culture upon which the planters will go are particularly indigo, hemp, flax, cotton, tobacco, vines, and silk, not to speak of Indian corn, wheat, and other provisions: for all these, it is said, no part of America can be better adapted.

It is very much to be wished, that so fine a tract of country may be put to the most advantageous use, particularly in respect of silk, wine, and hemp. These are commodities which we want more than any others from our colonies, but for want of a proper soil and climate the nation has for so many years been disappointed in its expectations; but there can be no doubt of all these articles doing as well in this newly-acquired country as in any part of the world, provided the right methods are

taken

taken in the culture of them. Planters left entirely to themselves are apt to fall into the articles of husbandry to which they have been most acquainted, and not into those which will pay them the greatest profit, unless they have been before acquainted with them. But their chusing their crops well is a matter of vast importance to this nation, and therefore proper means should be taken to give them all the light and instruction that is wanting in any thing which it would be adviseable for them to undertake. Persons skilled in feeding silk-worms and winding the silk should be distributed through every district of such a country; such might be got in America, and they should teach, gratis, every family that was willing to learn the business. The same thing should be done with vine-dressers from France, or perhaps better from Portugal, Spain, Italy, or Greece; these men should move from plantation to plantation, to shew the planters the culture of vineyards—to assist in planting them, and also in dressing the vineyard: it would not be very expensive to procure forty or fifty such; and that number would in a few years be able to train up many pupils, and spread a tolerable knowledge of the vineyard culture through two or three provinces. Hemp is better underſtood in America, the ſame means would not therefore be neceſſary. To theſe meaſures rewards, both honorary and pecuniary, ſhould be added, for ſuch planters as produced given quantities of the beſt wine, of ſilk, and of hemp: a couple of thouſand pounds a year beſtowed upon a province in ſuch premiums, would be ſufficient to introduce, in conjunction with the above mentioned meaſure, any article of culture the government would have them purſue; and nobody can doubt but the national intereſt would be far more advanced by ſuch an expenditure of public money, than injured by the loſs (ſuppoſing it ſuch) of a few thouſand pounds. There is ſcarcely any thing in domeſtic policy but what may be effected, and with profit, by means of premiums judiciouſly offered, and impartially given, provided means be at the ſame time taken to inſtruct the people, if the object required be out of their knowledge. Inſtead of acting thus, the bounty on ſilk has been ſuffered to expire.

Bounties and other encouragements of this nature have been of long ſtanding for hemp and other articles without effect; but this proves nothing in general. While the colon iſts colonists were confined to the coasts of America, by which I mean the flat, poor, sandy tract of country which extends for 100 or 150 miles from the sea, no encouragement would ever make any thing of hemp, silk, or wine, for the soil and climate were equally unfit for all; but now they have spread themselves into the back or hilly country, where both soil and climate are essentially different, the case is different also; and much less encouragement would prove of high utility, than before was attended with no effect. For this reason, the old inefficacy of such measures should never be instanced as an argument against them at present.

Very many great and beneficial effects might be made to flow from the settling and planting the internal parts of our maritime colonies. Hemp is an article which costs this nation several hundred thousand pounds annually: it is besides a necessary for our royal navy, which ought not to depend on the good pleasure of any foreign nation, whatever friendship may be between us at present.

Flax is another import which we take from the Baltic, though our colonies would raise it as well, and parts of them perhaps much better.

I have not seen public accounts of what our import of wines of all sorts is, but certainly it amounts to an immense sum; the wealth of the nation would be very different if such an import, chiefly from our own sworn enemies, was transferred to our colonies, and instead of being paid for with cash, as is the case with hemp, to be purchased with our manufactures.

Silk is another article which we import from China, at the expence of more than half a million sterling; yet our silk-mills are universal in affirming, that what we have had from America is equal to the best we receive elsewhere: surely therefore it much behoves the government to promote whatever measures have a tendency to render silk an article of consideration in the imports from America, instead of suffering old ones to expire.

Oil is another import which costs this country great sums of money: none is or can be produced at home; but the olive thrives well in the interior part of Georgia, and might be made a valuable article in the products of that province, especially the new acquired district.

Madder we buy of the Dutch, to the amount of more than two hundred thousand pounds a year; those industrious people

raise

raise it in the province of Zealand, that is, in a country far inferior in soil to the back parts of Georgia, where are tracts of rich deep black loam that would produce prodigious crops of it: no article of American husbandry would prove a more profitable staple.

Wool we take in large quantities of Spain, because it is of a kind we cannot produce in England: our colonies on the continent of North America, south of New York, produce a wool entirely similar to the Spanish; no staple they could produce would therefore be more advantageous to Great Britain. It is well known that a piece of fine broad cloth cannot be made without Spanish wool; it is also known that the Spaniards have of late years made great efforts to work up their own wool; if they should succeed, or if they should by any other means prevent the export of it, our woollen fabrics, though they might not be stopped, would at least be burthened with a fresh expence and new trouble; all which would be prevented by encouraging the import of wool from America; and at the same time that this good effect was wrought, another would be brought about in cramping the manufactures of the colonies; of which more hereafter.

Cotton we import from Turkey at the expence of above two hundred thousand pounds a year; this commodity agrees well with the soil and climate of Georgia, especially those of the back parts of the province: I am sensible that our West India islands would produce it, but the land which is so occupied there would produce more valuable staples; there we want land, but on the continent is more land than we know what to do with; it is here therefore that it should be produced.

These imports might be enlarged to a greater number, were it necessary, but they are sufficient to shew that the nation takes from foreign countries, and from enemies, commodities to a very great amount, which she might have produced in her colonies. It is at present the opinion of many mercantile gentlemen, that the balance of all our trades, except America and the East Indies, is against us; if so, it must undeniably be owing in a great measure to the great consumption of these articles, many of which are taken from countries that take little from us: if our colonies produced them, we should, on the contrary,

pay

pay for them with our manufactures, a circumstance essentially different from having them in any other mode.

A writer who has taken great pains to be well informed, has given the following account of some of these imports.

	£.
Hemp and flax, - - -	400,000
Wine and brandy from France alone in 1663,	100,000
Suppose the total - - -	1,000,000
Ireland alone in one article, claret, takes 150,000l.	
Silk, - - - -	1,825,000
Cotton, - - - -	* 300,000
Madder other accounts make	250,000
Let us suppose oil - - -	50,000
And for wool - - -	50,000
Total	3,875,000

Other imports, which do not concern so immediately our *southern* colonies, as iron, timber, &c. &c. would run this account up to a much greater height: but if the total did not amount to more than half of it, surely the sum is too considerable to take from foreign nations, in articles which we might produce generally as well in our own colonies.

---

* *Political Essays concerning the present State of the British Empire*, 1771.

CHAP.

CHAP. XXVI.

EAST FLORIDA.

False descriptions of the country—Climate—Soil—Productions—Observations.

WEST FLORIDA.

Climate — Soil — Importance of these provinces relative to situation and commerce— Observations.

IN such a free country as Britain, new acquisitions made at a peace will not be well understood for some years. The party who concludes the treaty will in the nature of things extol the terms they have gained, and for that purpose magnify the acquisitions they have made: on the other hand, the party in opposition will be sure to condemn the treaty, and depreciate the value of the territories acquired; and what is a great misfortune in such a case, is the almost universal influence of parties: few men that actually go to the countries in question, but whose judgment or report will be
warped

warped by their connections or political opinions. Most of the people who frequent such countries are soldiers, sailors, governors, civil officers, or traders, and if any of these should publish accounts, not much strict truth is always met with in their descriptions; either from being fearful to offend their superiors, or from motives of interest. It happened thus with the Floridas. The ministry, upon the conclusion of the peace, sent a physician, who had no business to leave in England, to view and describe East Florida; though upon his return he found his employers out of office, and a new administration, yet as his was an official business, he dedicated his book to the minister of the day: it contained an account of that province, which made it appear to be one of the finest countries in the world, and proved it a most valuable acquisition. This was just the report which the world might rationally have expected; for certainly a man on such an errand would take care, first to recommend himself to his patrons, which he could do no ways so effectually as by praising the acquisitions they had made to the skies: in this work, indeed, he did not proceed on those principles of integrity which he ought to have done.

done. An American botanist accompanied him in a part of his journey through the province, and kept a journal; this made a part of the above-mentioned publication; but instead of being published fairly, it was mangled, and the man's general opinion of the country, which was by no means favourable to it, suppressed. Such a conduct, at one stroke, was sufficient to convince the reader that little or no dependance could be placed in what was advanced by a man who could prove, in so material an instance, faithless to the public.

On the other hand, direct contrary accounts were published by others, who were so far from agreeing to the merit of the country set forth by its friends, that they strenuously insisted it had no pretensions to any sort of merit: they totally denied all value to it, ridiculed the title of acquisition, considered the country as a heavy burthen, and condemned the peace-makers with the loudest voice, for accepting such a recompense in exchange for glorious and valuable conquests made in the war. Here therefore were two parties in such direct opposition to each other, that a considerable part of what they wrote might fairly be attributed to political prejudice; and this on both

both sides, the consequence of which was, that the world could form but a very vague guess of the real truth.

Such is the state of public intelligence concerning the Floridas; all the information to be gained concerning them, is that of private people who have resided there: I have been as attentive as possible in making numerous enquiries, of planters, agents, officers, &c. who have been any time in those countries; I have compared their accounts, and from the intelligence I have gained, have drawn up the following description, supplying some deficiencies by reasoning from analogy of Georgia and Carolina, and others from public accounts, of a date antecedent to our having any connection with Florida, and consequently free from all party prejudice. The account will be incomplete, as the sources from which it is drawn are so; but it had much better be incomplete than otherwise, if to make it so, bad intelligence, or such as was unsatisfactory, was taken to render it full. In a few particulars (wherein it would answer little purpose in him to vary from the truth), I follow Dr. Stork.

East Florida is situated between lat. 25 and 32, it extends consequently much to
the

the south of any of our other colonies, which makes the climate hotter; a considerable part of it forms a peninsula, which projects to the south: this circumstance is both an advantage and a disadvantage; in the first place, it makes the air cooler by a regular sea and land breeze, than in the maritime part of Georgia; but on the other hand, this benefit is almost preponderated by the increased quantiiy of rain which falls; it is the mischief of all these southern coasts of America, that they are deluged with rain, which, stagnating in the swamps of a flat hot country, poisons the air. The rains that fall in Florida are almost incessant. This in a hot climate must make it very unhealthy, since those are the wholesomest countries near the tropics, where it seldom rains. Peru is perfectly healthy, and there it never rains at all. Relative to the health and fertility of this country, there is one circumstance that is decisive; all the southern colonies I have elsewhere remarked, consist of a maritime and a back country, the latter of which reaches to the Apalachean mountains; now the flat sandy coast, full of swamps and marshes, is alike in them all, being equally steril and unwholesome; but when this flat

flat country is passed, and you arrive at the hilly dry tracts, free from swamps, you then find a country perfectly healthy, and very fruitful. Florida, Georgia, the Carolinas, Virginia, and Maryland, are all extremely similar in the appearance of their coasts; the flat sandy tract is the same in them all, except that their small degree of fertility increases as you advance northward, as regularly as the arrangement of the colonies. Now this circumstance is absolutely decisive against East Florida, for unfortunately, that province consists of nothing else but the flat sandy country; it has no back country, for where you should meet with the rising drier tract, you come to the swamps and marshes of West Florida; therefore not a hill is to be met with in the whole province: it consists of marshes after marshes, swamps after swamps, pine barrens upon pine barrens, but no sound good loam like the hiccory lands in the back parts of Georgia, &c. Indeed the general spontaneous produce of the province shews us what the soil is. Good lands in this part of America are covered with woods of tall red hiccories as high and straight as elms; white, chesnut, and scarlet oaks; tulip trees; black walnuts; locusts, &c.

But single trees of these are rare in East Florida, and not a wood of them is to be found in the whole province.

Now these two circumstances are such as can neither be mistaken nor misunderstood; the flat situation of the country, and the spontaneous produce; the one may be in a small degree remedied by the sea and land breezes; and small patches of tolerable (not good) land may be quoted in answer to the other; but as to the country in general, it must be condemned on comparison with very great tracts in our old colonies. This I must own appears to me to be clearly deducible from the circumstances in question; party on either side cannot alter or deceive one in such points, because they are certainly matters of fact, and not opinion; nor could there well be a greater piece of imposition on the public, than publishing the direct contrary.

Relative to the soil and face of the country, it resembles, as I before observed, the maritime parts of the other southern colonies: it consists chiefly of swamps and marshes, or tracts of sandy white pine ground; the former are covered with the spontaneous growth of the country, live oaks, chinkapins, bays, liquid amber, water

ter oaks, and stunted cypresses. In fertility for the product of rice, there are some of them which it is imagined will answer well; when the swamps more to the north are exhausted or turned to meadow, which, however, is not likely ever to be the case; and therefore the merit of this capability is not of much consequence: the swamps we were in possession of, before the acquisition of Florida was made, would, if cultivated, produce more rice than half the world consumes.

The rest of the country is in general a pine barren, with very small spots of better land, which the Indians of Florida formerly grew their maize on: now the pine barren is the worst land of America, but to say that it is absolutely sterile, would be asserting an untruth; for no soil can be such in a climate that is very wet and very hot, since those two agents will every where make the worst of land produce something: this pine barren will, when cleared, produce indigo, Indian corn, and some other crops; but then it is not the proper soil for any one of them, and such as no person would move to, from the worst of our colonies, in order to cultivate them. This seems to be the plain fact, when cleared from the attendants which prejudice has given it. The country will produce rice and indigo, and a few other unimportant articles; but the culture will not by any means be so advantageous as the same articles in Carolina.

Several plantations have been formed, stocked with negroes, and set to work on rice, indigo, Indian corn, sugar, cotton, hemp, and cochineal. Among these the plantations of Mr. Rolle, governor Grant, the earl of Egmont, and Mr. Taylor, are the principal; none of these have been able to bring any dubious article of culture into profit, such as sugar, cotton, cochineal, hemp, &c. on the contrary, had they not depended on rice and indigo, they would have lost their whole capital, and with the assistance of those articles, which in Carolina, are almost uniformly profitable, they have most of them lost such large sums of money, as to break up some of the plantations, and give no slight languor to them all. The description published of the province induced many to set about planting; they expected returns of sugar, cotton, cochineal, and hemp, and made little doubt of soon acquiring great fortunes: all they met with was disappointment on disap-

disappointment; this chagrined them, and perhaps they were then little inclined to do even justice to their own beginnings. But all men who have any ideas of planting in America, whether by going thither themselves, or under the conduct of agents, should consider well the country which they chuse. Had the gentlemen who have laid out large sums in planting Florida considered what the country probably was, from reasoning by analogy with Georgia, Carolina, &c. they would presently have perceived that it would have been more advantageous to settle in the back parts of our old colonies, than in our new acquisitions of the Floridas.

In respect to West Florida, we have a little intelligence which can be depended on, as it is principally of an older date than our acquisition of it. The whole coast has been well known ever since the year 1719, and the many accounts the French have given of it, to be nothing but such a sandy desart; "the land is nothing but a fine sand, as white and shining as snow [*]." This is the account they give of the country from the Mississippi to Mobile; of

---

[*] Du Pratz Hist. de Louis. l. 52.

which last an officer of twenty years experience in the country gives his opinion in these words: " I never could see for what reason this fort was built, or what could be the use of it; although it is 120 leagues from New Orleans, it must be supplied from thence; the soil is so bad, being nothing but sand, that it produces nothing but pine trees, or a little pulse, which is but indifferent of the kind *." They only settled there for the sake of a port in Dauphin isle, and which was choaked up by the shifting of the sands in a gale of wind, and leaves the place without any port above the depth of nine feet. Their other settlements on this coast, they tell us, " only deserved an oblivion as lasting as their duration was short." They then took Pensacola from the Spaniards, but found it only fit to dismantle and abandon; on which they retired to the Mississippi, as we must do if ever we would hold that country. The greatest part of Florida was surveyed in 1708, by Captain Mairn from Carolina, who gives this account of it for about an hundred miles square round Pensacola. " All this country is a *pine barren* (sandy

---

* *Du Mont. Mem. de la Louis.* tom. ii. p. 80.

desart),

desart), without any water in it;" that is, it has neither earth nor water in it, and must therefore be very unfit for a *plantation*. All the rest appears to be the same where it is not swampy and marshy. We may say of the whole, what Father Charlevoix, who travelled all over it, says of the next post at St. Joseph's, which lies in the middle of the country upon the borders of East and West Florida, " it is a wretched country *(un pays perdu)*, and a mere barren sand, on a flat and bleak sea-coast—the last place on earth where one would expect to meet with any mortal, and above all with christians*." The following account was wrote by an officer from Pensacola, and has been confirmed by other eye-witnesses. " My expectations with regard to this country, and the hopes of every one else, are sunk to the lowest pitch. Instead of the finest country in the world (as West Florida was called), we found the most sandy, barren, and desart land, that eyes could see or imagination paint! not capable of producing a single vegetable, nor the least prospect of improving it! as the soil for an hundred miles back is every where

---

* *Hist. N. France*, vi. p. 263.

the same as the sea-shore, and consists not of earth but of the whitest sand you ever saw;" which agrees with the account of Capt. Mairn above. " In summer it is too hot to go abroad in the day time; the months of July, August, and September, are said to be as hot as at Jamaica. The winter is very cold; but as it depends on what wind blows, that is very uncertain. You have often contrary extremes in the same day; a south wind scorches, and a north wind freezes, which must be very disagreeable. There is so much sickness at Mobile, that almost all the officers are ill, and only sixty men of a regiment able to do duty;" which was afterwards the case at Pensacola.

This is the first part of North America that was ever attempted to be settled, and has been better known than any part of the continent, although it seems now to be almost unknown and forgotten. It was first undertaken to be settled by John Ponce in 1512; Vasquez d'Ayllon in 1520, and 1524; Pamphilo Navarez, who had a grant of it in 1528; Fernando Soto from 1539 to 1541; a company of missionaries in 1549; Pedro de Melendez, who had a grant of all the southern parts of North America

America in 1562 to 1586; the French under Ribault and Laudonniere from 1562 to 1567; but they all found the country to be so poor and barren, that they abandoned it, insomuch that it has never been settled as a colony to this day. Soto travelled all over the western parts of the peninsula, from the bay of Spirito Santo, where he landed, and tells us from that to the inland parts of Georgia, " that country which is no less than 350 leagues in extent, is a light and soft sand, full of swamps, and very high and thick bushes, which is very poor and barren;" but where lands bear nothing but bushes or underwoods in America, they are good for nothing. Narvaez again searched all the eastern and inland parts for 280 leagues, " and found it to be all a low flat sand, full of swamps, with a sad and dismal aspect throughout the whole country." " Solum omne quod hactenus lustraverant (secundum ipsorum calculum 280 leucarum) planum erat atque arenosum multis stagnis riguum—Tristem & squallidam regionis faciem renuntiavit *."

---

* *De Laet.* l. iv. c. 3. *Herrera,* dec. iv. l. 4 c 4.

From all these accounts, and from all the authentic documents with which the council of the Indies in Spain could furnish him, which were numerous, the historian of America again informs us, " Florida is a poor country, without any commodity but a few sorry pearls, and all who ever went to it died in misery *."

The bounds of both the Floridas were settled by proclamation in the autumn of 1763: they extend northwards, the east province to the limits of Georgia, and the west to the 31st degree of north latitude: now it is to be remarked, that the barren noxious country just described on various authorities, extends a very little farther than lat. 31, for when you come to Manchac on the Mississippi the high lands begin, and a country in every respect the reverse of West Florida. Those accounts and writings therefore which represent this country in a favourable light, must undoubtedly have reference only to the tract of high country beyond the *new* limits of the province. I shall hereafter shew that that country is one of the finest in the world.

---

* *Present State of Great Britain and North America*, p. 197.
* *Herrera*, dec. iii. l. 8. c. 8.

The description here given of the two Floridas may be supposed to carry a strong condemnation of that article in the peace of Paris, which gave to Spain an object of vast value in return for a province, which apparently was not worth the expence of keeping; but the same impartiality which was my guide in describing the climate and soil, obliges me to declare, that this idea would not be so just as it may at first sight appear: if Florida was accepted with a view only for cultivation and colonizing upon the same principles as other colonies, I should agree that the remark would be undeniably just, but the matter may reasonably be put in a quite different light. Florida was an acquisition worth making, upon the principles of removing a dangerous neighbour, and acquiring the possession of a coast equally well situated for cramping, in case of war, the commerce of the Spanish colonies, or carrying on a clandestine trade with them. When Georgia was settled with a view to rendering it a frontier against the enemy, and when general Oglethorpe executed the expedition against St. Augustine, had he succeeded in it, and conquered the whole of the two Floridas, we should then have had pens in plenty to prove

prove the importance of the country: considered in this light it is of importance; at St. Augustine the Spaniards were dangerous enemies, and would have continued so till Georgia became far more populous than it is at present; they also afforded a retreat to runaway negroes, which was a great inconvenience. The point of carrying on a clandestine trade with the Spanish colonies is more important; this may be judged of by the fact of the imports from West Florida, amounting soon after the peace, and notwithstanding Mr. Grenville's preposterous regulations, to the annual sum of 63,000 l. in Spanish dollars, a sum superior to what was received from Georgia thirty years after settling at an immense expence, and is an earnest of what may in future be expected, if a more politic conduct is pursued.

That the possession of so great an extent of coast, bounding a streight, through which the Spanish galleons have their course, may prove, in case of war, a very valuable acquisition, cannot be denied; for by means of the ports this coast yields us, we may be able to cruize for the enemies ships with much greater probability of success, than we ever had before in this part of the world.

world. Nor should it be forgotten that the possession of these provinces renders our dominion in North America complete; the whole territory of that continent, east of the Mississippi, is now entirely ours; the course of that river is now open to us to its mouth, a matter perhaps of more consequence in future than all the other points I have mentioned, and which we could not have had securely without the joint cession of Florida, and the eastern Louisiana; there is a roundness now in our continental dominions which will save our posterity, if not ourselves, no slight expences.

That these are circumstances of merit, can be denied by none but men who are determined to judge and condemn compendiously, and without the trouble of discrimination; but such general and concise determinations are seldom founded in that degree of accuracy and truth which a candid enquirer will naturally demand. How far the country is adequate to the reasonable expectations of the kingdom—for the great sacrifices made for it, is another equiry, not fit to be made at present, while the parties who made the peace, and those who opposed it are yet living, and their politics yet the signal for arrangement

ment in party matters; nor is such an enquiry so nearly connected with the subject of this work, as the objects which I have principally treated of. What I have laid before the reader is sufficient to shew that the rational plan of proceeding with relation to these provinces, is to secure the coasts by a few strong and well situated fortresses, that the country may be safe from the attacks of enemies, and that there may be the proper accommodations for shipping, for the views of attack in time of war, and trade in time of peace; as to planting, none should be encouraged but such as was subordinate to the design of supplying the garrisons and shipping. By no encouragement, however, I do not mean restrictions, but avoiding those public means of bringing new settlers, which are often put in execution: such people will be employed to far more national purposes in other parts of our colonies, which exceed Florida equally in health and fertility. As the strength of the Spaniards is now collected at New Orleans, and as the navigation of the Mississippi is much the most important object we have in this part of the world, the government should be particularly attentive to keeping all the forts,

forts, stations, and fortresses in that part of the province in the best condition, that in case of a rupture with Spain, we might there be secure. When the new colony of the Ohio comes to flourish, in that manner which it certainly will in a few years, the infinite importance of this object will be striking to every one; nor should we forget the noble tract of fertile country we have on the banks of the Mississippi, which will one day or other be among the most important parts of all America, and which will almost entirely depend on the undisturbed enjoyment of the free navigation of that river.

CHAP.

CHAP. XXVII.

EASTERN LOUISIANA.

Territory eastward of the Mississippi—Climate — Soil— Great fertility — Productions—Cattle—Face of the country — Staples produced here by the French—Proposed colony—Observations.

I Give the name of Eastern Louisiana to the tract of country on the east side of the river Mississippi, from the boundary of West Florida to the forks of that river, formed by its junction with the Ohio. This country reaches from lat. 31 and $\frac{1}{2}$ to lat. 37 and $\frac{1}{2}$; and from east to west I extend it to the countries of the Chicasaw, Cherokee, and Creek Indians, which is about the distance of from 150 to 300 miles; this space being entirely free from the habitations, huntings, and claims of the Indians, having been in the undisturbed possession of the French till their cession of it to Great Britain, and settled and planted at various places according to the inclinations of the individuals, who came from France

or

or Canada. The country weſt of the river is that part of Louiſiana which they retained, and afterwards ceded to the Spaniards.

This territory was left as hunting ground for the Indians in the proclamation, which ſettled the bounds of our colonies, in 1763, an arrangement which has ſince been juſtly and ſeverely condemned; ſince it was in this inſtance, as well as in that of the Ohio, the giving up the beſt countries acquired by the late war, at the ſame time that we planted the worſt. But as I conceive that this territory of the Miſſiſſippi will come in a few years to be ſettled and planted, from the ſame cogent reaſons which have at laſt induced the government to allow the ſettlement of the Ohio, I think it will be highly proper to give the beſt deſcription of it that can be procured, in thoſe circumſtances which relate to agriculture. I am the rather induced to do this, as I have it in my power, from the information I have received from an ingenious gentleman of South Carolina, and likewiſe from two officers, all of whom either travelled through, or reſided in the country, to lay before the reader a few circumſtances not ſufficiently known before.

Their

Their intelligence also enables me to distinguish, in the accounts that have been published of the country, facts from errors and mistakes.

Relative to the climate of this country it resembles that of the back territories of Carolina, near the mountains, but is at the same time generally allowed to be better and more healthy; particularly in the circumstance of not being so hot in summer, nor so cold in winter. The whole territory enjoys much such a temperature as the best parts of Spain: the air is clear, dry, and pure, perfectly free from all mists and fogs. This quality is much owing to the country being remarkably high and dry; in general from one to two hundred feet higher than the river in its greatest floods: there is not a swamp or a marsh in the whole country; no stinking unhealthy effluvia to thicken and poison the air, which in so considerable a tract of our colonies is destruction to the health of the inhabitants. The heats here are very seldom oppressive, from the dryness of the air; and instead of the incessant and heavy rains which surprise Europeans in Carolina, Georgia, and Florida, it on the contrary seldom rains on the Mississippi, north of the bounds of West Florida,

Florida, that is, in the high country. This circumstance is very valuable, not upon account of healthiness only, but for several valuable articles of cultivation, particularly silk and wine. The reader cannot attend too much to the climate of this country, because very essential interests will by and by depend on it; whenever the proposition to settle it is made, objections may perhaps arise on account of climate, and new tales in support of Lords of *Trade*, who oppose *plantations*; but let the world then recollect the accounts which have been long ago given of this province, and which in every circumstance of climate has been uniformly described by every person that has been there. Had the countries which have been of late years colonized (particularly Nova Scotia and the Floridas) been described in a just and true manner, in all the circumstances of climate and soil, errors which have been made might not have happened. But with relation to the tracts of country on the Mississippi, all travellers, residents, writers, &c. agree in one general and uniform voice, all describe the climate as being perfectly wholesome, free from excessive and oppressive heats, from fogs, damps, rains,

and

and such intense colds, as are felt on the coast of Carolina in the same latitude. In all these respects, no country can be more truly desirable.

The soil of this country is not at all inferior to the climate. Du Pratz, who resided sixteen years in Louisiana, and eight of them at the post at Natchez, and who from his profession of a planter must necessarily be a judge of land, speaks of it in terms, that leave one nothing to doubt. From that part of it to the Ohio, which is about 900 miles, the slope of the lands goes off perpendicularly from the Mississippi, being on the banks of that river, from one to two hundred feet high. All these high lands are, besides, surmounted in a good many places, by little eminences or small hills, and rising grounds, running off lengthwise with gentle slopes. It is only when we go a little way from the Mississippi that we find these high-lands are over-topped by little mountains, which appear to be all of earth though steep, without the least gravel or pebble being perceived on them. The soil, continues he, on these high lands is very good. It is a black light mould, about three feet deep, on the hills or rising grounds: this upper earth
lies

lies upon a reddish clay, very strong and stiff; the lowest places between these hills are of the same nature, but there the black earth is between five and six feet deep. The grass growing in the hollows is of the height of a man, and very slender and fine; whereas the grass of the same meadow on the high lands rises scarce knee deep, as it does on the highest eminences. All these lands are either meadows or forests of tall trees, with grass up to the knee; the timber is oak, hiccory, mulberry, &c. Even reeds and canes grow on the hill sides, tho' they are found in our maritime colonies only in the richest swamps.

All the accounts we have had, both public and private, agree in these circumstances, and nothing can be more decisive of the excellency of the lands in this country. In the southern parts of this continent grass is very scarce every where but on the richest lands; insomuch that it is no unsatisfactory proof of the soil being good to find a plenty of any grass, much more such a luxuriant produce of it as is met with even on the hills of this country. The trees are no less indications of what the nature of the land is, being such as are

only

only found on good soils, and of a size and straitness met with alone on the very richest.

Charlevoix, who from the vast extent of his travels was no stranger to these appearances of various kinds which denote good land, and in general a fine country, has several particulars which it is proper to transcribe: speaking of his entrance into this country from the north, he says, "There is not, in my opinion, a place in all Louisiana more proper for a settlement than the fork at the junction of the Mississippi and the Ohio, nor where it is of greater importance to have one; the whole country watered by the Ouabache and Ohio, which runs into it, is extremely fertile, consisting of vast meadows." A later writer, of our own country, makes the same remark: "the most important place in this country, and perhaps in all North America, is at the forks of the Mississippi, where the Ohio falls into that river, which, like another ocean, is the general receptacle of all the rivers that water the interior parts of that vast continent. Here those large and navigable rivers, the Ohio, the Cherokee river, Illionois, Missouri, and Mississippi, besides many others which spread over that whole

whole continent, from the Apalachean mountains to the mountains of New Mexico, upwards of a thousand miles both north, south, east, and west, all meet together at this spot; and that in the best climate and one of the most fruitful countries of any in all that part of the world; in the latitude 37°, the latitude of the capes of Virginia, and of Sante Fé, the capital of New Mexico. By that means there is a convenient navigation to this place from our present settlements to New Mexico, and from all the inland parts of North America, farther than we are acquainted with it; and all the natives of that continent have by that means a free and ready access to this place. In short, this place is in the center of that vast continent, and of all the nations in it, and seems to be intended by nature to command them both; for which reason it ought no longer to be neglected by Britain.

"Upon the neighbourhood of the Chisaw river, Charlevoix remarks, that the country is delightful; the meadows preserve their verdure in the winter, and a considerable number of well-wooded islands in the Mississippi, some of which are pretty large, form very beautiful canals, through which

which the largest ships may safely pass; it being affirmed that there is sixty fathom water in the Mississippi above 150 leagues from the sea. As to the forests, which almost entirely cover this immense country, there is nothing perhaps in nature comparable to them, whether we consider the size and height of the trees, or their variety and the advantages which may be drawn from them; for excepting dying woods, which require a warmer soil, and are only to be met with between the tropics, there is hardly any sort of trees which can be mentioned that are not to be found here. There are forests of cypress eight or ten leagues in extent, all the trees of which are of a thickness proportioned to their height, surpassing every thing we have of that kind in France. That sort of ever-green laurel, which we have called the tulip-tree on account of the shape of its flower, is now beginning to be known in Europe. This grows to a greater height than the chesnut-tree of India, and its leaf is much more beautiful. The canton of Natchez is the finest, most fertile, and best peopled of all Louisiana; it lies at the distance of about forty leagues from the Yazows, upon the same side of the river. Several little hills appear above th fort,

which

which is called Rosalie, and when these are once passed, we see on all sides very large meadows, separated from one another by small thickets of wood, which produce a very fine effect. The trees most common in these woods are the oak, and those which produce nuts: the soil is every where excellent. The late Monf. d'Iberville, who first entered the Mississippi by its mouth, having penetrated so far up as the Natchez, found the country so delightful and so advantageously situated, that he concluded the metropolis of the new colony could no where be better placed. If ever Louisiana becomes a flourishing colony, as it may very well happen, it is my opinion there cannot be a better situation for a capital than this. It is not liable to be overflowed by the river, has a very pure air, and a great extent of country; the soil is well watered, and capable of producing every thing. Nor is it at too great a distance from the sea, and there is nothing to prevent shipping from going up to it. Lastly, it is at a convenient distance from all those places where there can be any design of making settlements."

The reader will remark, that these several accounts are perfectly consistent; it is evident from them that all this country, to the east of the Mississippi, is one of the finest in the world in respect of climate and soil; the air is pleasant and healthy, the heats are never oppressive, nor the frosts injurious; the atmosphere is clear and dry, and free from the impurities with which it is loaded in countries abounding with marshes and swamps: the circumstance of the face of the country being high, and either hilly or sloping off in gradual ascents, and the soil at the same time deep and rich, is uncommon and particularly valuable; for great fertility in such healthy regions is by no means generally found. The spontaneous productions are also such as give the most perfect satisfaction, whether taken as mere indications of what the soil is, or for their native value. Some of them have been mentioned, but others are equally deserving attention.

Among these I shall first mention the vine, which, says Du Pratz, is so common in Louisiana, that whatever way you walk from the sea-coast for 500 leagues northwards, you cannot proceed an hundred steps without meeting with one; but unless the vine-shoots should happen to grow in an exposed place, it cannot be expected that
their

their fruit should ever come to perfect maturity. The trees to which they twine are so high, and so thick of leaves, and the intervals of underwood are so filled with reeds, that the sun cannot warm the earth or ripen the fruit of this shrub. On the edge of the savannahs or meadows we meet with a grape, the shoots of which resemble those of the Burgundy grape: they make from this a tolerable good wine, if they take care to expose it to the sun in summer, and to the cold in winter. I have made this experiment myself, and must say, that I could never turn it into vinegar. There is another kind of grape which I make no difficulty of classing with the grapes of Corinth, commonly called currants. If it were planted and cultivated in an open field, I make not the least doubt but it would equal that grape. Muscadine grapes, of an amber colour, of a very good kind and very sweet, have been found upon declivities of a good exposure, even so far north as the latitude of 31 degrees. There is the greatest probability that they might make excellent wine of these, as it cannot be doubted but the grapes might be brought to great perfection in this country, since in the moist soil of New Orleans the cuttings

tings of the grape, which some of the inhabitants of that city brought from France, have succeeded extremely well, and afforded good wine.

Mulberries are found in vast plenty in most parts of the country. They have great numbers and a variety of kinds of walnuts and hiccories, and large chesnut-trees, which however do not grow in plenty within 100 leagues of the sea. Of the common forest timber, the red cedar is the most valuable; it is found in great plenty. Next to it ranks the cypress; it is reckoned incorruptible; one was found twenty feet deep in the earth, near New Orleans, uncorrupted. Now the lands of Lower Louisiana have been found to be augmented two leagues every century; this tree therefore must have been buried at least twelve centuries. Boats called *pettiaugres* are made of single trunks of this tree, that will carry three or four thousand weight, and sometimes more. Of one of these trees a carpenter made two, one of which carried sixteen ton, and the other fourteen. The pines are only found on the sandy tracts on the sea-coast. The sassafras is here a large and tall tree. The myrtle wax tree is found in plenty, and its wax was always one

one of the principal articles in the exports from New Orleans. The locuſt *(acacia)* is found on all the higher lands, and is a ſtrong ſign of a good ſoil. The mangrove is found in ſome parts of the country. Among their oaks they have the ever-green one and the red; it is well known that the beſt ſhips built in America are thoſe which have their timbers of ever-green oak, and their plank of cedar; and it is aſſerted that the red oak of Louiſiana is as good as the ever-green one. The aſh, elm, beech, lime, hornbeam, aſp willow, alder, &c. are the ſame as in Europe. Sarſaparilla grows naturally in Louiſiana, and it is not inferior in its qualities to that of Mexico. Hops grow naturally in the gullies in the high lands. The canes or reeds grow to vaſt height; one kind comes in moiſt places to eighteen feet, and the thickneſs of the wriſt. The natives make mats, ſieves, ſmall boxes, and other works of it. Thoſe that grow in dry places, are neither ſo high nor ſo thick, but are ſo hard, that, before the arrival of the French, the natives uſed ſplits of theſe canes to cut their victuals with. After a certain number of years the large canes bear a great abundance of grain, which is ſomewhat like oats, but about

about three times as large. The natives carefully gather those grains, and make bread or gruel of them. This flour swells as much as that of wheat. When the reeds have yielded the grain they die, and none appear for a long time after in the same place, especially if fire has been set to the old ones. Hemp grows naturally in this country; the stalks are as thick as one's finger, and about six feet long: they are quite like ours, both in the wood, the leaf, and the rind. The flax which was sown in this country rose three feet high.—The reader cannot well have greater satisfaction relative to the high importance of this country, than the preceding recapitulation of part of its natural produce. The productions of agriculture will not be found to speak less effectually to the same purpose.

Maize was not only cultivated by the Indians in small quantities for their subsistence during a part of the year, but also by the French as an article of considerable exportation to the sugar islands: it was here found to thrive better on a black and light earth than on a strong one. Such as began plantations of it in the woods, thick set with cane, found an advantage in the maize which made amends for the labour

of

of clearing the ground; a labour always more fatiguing than cultivating a spot already cleared. The advantage was this; they began with cutting down the canes for a great extent of ground; the trees they peeled two feet high quite round. This operation they performed the beginning of March, as then the sap is in motion in that country: about fifteen days after the canes being dry, were set on fire, and burnt, burning or at least killing the trees with them. The following day they sowed the maize, in squares four feet asunder; the roots of the canes which are not quite dead shoot out fresh canes, which are very tender and brittle, and as no other weeds grow in the field that year, it is easy to be weeded of these canes, and as much corn again used to be made in this manner as in a field already cultivated.

Wheat, rye, barley, oats, pease, and beans of many sorts thrive no where in the world better than on the high lands in this country, in every spot where the French planted them, and yielded a produce much greater without manure than can be gained in common lands in Europe with great manuring: the temperature of the climate suits wheat extraordinarily, and no soil can
be

be better adapted to it. But in Lower Louisiana upon the coast, which is the same country as West Florida, the French found that it would not thrive at all.

Indigo was commonly cultivated in this country, than which none more favourable, either in climate or soil, is any where to be found: the high lands produce it naturally. In the islands from the heat of climate they cut it four times; three good cuttings are had in Louisiana, of as good a quality at least, and producing as much as their four. In the particulars before given, concerning indigo in Carolina, I shewed that this plant required a rich, deep, black, dry loam, which is scarcely any where to be found in such perfection and plenty as in the country on the east of the Mississippi. No where in all North America will this staple be cultivated with so much success as here: the lands on the Ohio are as rich in many parts, but the climate is not so warm, being hardly warm enough for cultivating this plant with great success. Indigo is highly profitable both to the planter and the nation; it will therefore be found, whenever this noble country is colonized, that it must be one of the chief staples of it, and the crops
which

which will be here raised will certainly induce the people on the barren unhealthy coasts of our old colonies to quit them, and settle here, where their profit will prove very different, and they will thereby advance the interests of Britain as much as of themselves.

Hemp, I before observed, grows wild in Louisiana; but upon the eastern banks of the river, for a long way, there are very few tracts of low, marshy, strong land, such as hemp delights in, the lands being in general high and dry; that quantities might be made on the deep black mould, I doubt not, and perhaps if it was tried, it would not be found to require so much moisture; but, as upon the Ohio, hemp is also found spontaneous; and as the country is more various, having some tracts of low moist land on a strong clay, which would do admirably for this plant, and in which is found great natural crops; for this reason hemp might be considered as a staple for the Ohio, and the rich dry lands of the Mississippi applied to those crops which will only thrive in such.

Tobacco is another plant indigenous in this part of America; the French colonists cultivated it with such success that had

they

they received any encouragement from their government they might soon have rivalled Virginia and Maryland; but instead of this they were taxed heavily for cultivating it, by duties laid on the trade; what they produced was of so excellent a quality, as to sell some at five shillings a pound. This was raised in the country about Fort Rosalie, and to Yasouz. And there is one advantage in this culture here which ought not to be forgotten: in Louisiana the French planters, after the tobacco was cut, weeded and cleaned the ground on which it grew, the roots push forth fresh shoots, which are managed in the same manner as the first crop. By this means a second crop is made on the same ground, and sometimes a third. These *seconds* indeed, as they are called, do not usually grow so high as the first plant, but notwithstanding they make very good tobacco. Whereas in Virginia and Maryland the planters are prohibited by law from cultivating these *seconds*; the summers are there too short to bring them to maturity, but in Louisiana the summers are two or three months longer, by which means two or three crops of tobacco may be made in a year, as easily as one in Virginia. And a very

very experienced perfon in the tobacco trade affures us, that the frefh lands on the Miffiffippi will produce thrice or four times as much per working hand as our old plantations in Virginia and Maryland. This is perfectly confiftent with the beft accounts we have received from thence, which agree in defcribing the foil as very rich and very deep, of a black colour, and light and dry; fuch a foil is of a boundlefs fertility from its depth; where there is only a thin ftratum, though the richnefs may be great for a time, yet fucceffive crops of exhaufting plants will wear it out in no great number of years; but when the foil is, like that on the country on the eaft of the Miffiffippi, the fame for three, four, or five feet deep, the planter has nothing to fear. Every circumftance that is neceffary to fuccefs in tobacco planting is found in this territory. Firft, the right foil is the greateft plenty. Second, very extenfive tracts of fertile meadow, covered with the moft luxuriant grafs, for the maintenance of immenfe herds of cattle. Third, a navigation clofe to the tobacco lands, which admits fhips of five hundred tons. Fourth, a climate much better for this culture than that of

Vol. II.   G   our

our tobacco colonies. If all these circumstances are duly confidered, it will be found, that whenever the tobacco trade declines, or threatens a decline, the wife conduct will be to plant it in a country fo highly favourable to the bufinefs.

Silk may be produced in this country in any quantities that the population will allow of; for the mulberry is found in great plenty all over the high lands. The leaves of the natural mulberry-trees of Louifiana are what the filk-worms are very fond of; I mean the more common mulberries with a large leaf, but tender, and the fruit of the colour of Burgundy wine. The province produces alfo the white mulberry, which has the fame quality with the red. Du Pratz has a very juft obfervation on making filk in this country. " The culture, fays he, of indigo, tobacco, cotton, &c. may be carried on without any interruption to the making of filk, as any one of thefe is no manner of hindrance to the other. In the firft place, the work about thefe three plants does not come on till after the worms have fpun their filk: in the fecond place, the feeding and cleaning the filk-worm requires no great degree of ftrength; and thus the care employed
about

about them, interrupts no other sort of work either as to time or as to the persons employed therein. It suffices to have for this operation a person who knows how to feed and clean the worms; young negroes of both sexes might assist this person, little skill sufficing for this purpose; the oldest of the young negroes, when taught, might shift the worms and lay the leaves; the other young negroes gather and fetch them; and all this labour, which takes not up the whole day, lasts only for about six weeks. It appears therefore that the profit made of the silk is an additional benefit, so much the more profitable as it diverts not the workmen from their ordinary tasks. If it be objected, that buildings are requisite to make silk to advantage; I answer, buildings for the purpose cost very little in a country where wood may be had for taking; I add further, that these buildings may be made and daubed with mud by any persons about the family, and besides may serve for hanging tobacco in, two months after the silk-worms are gone."

There is another circumstance in which the high lands of this country are peculiarly adapted to the culture of silk, which is the dryness of the climate. Upon the maritime parts of our old colonies, the continual rains are very detrimental to this tender worm, which requires a fine healthy climate, as much as a man of a tender conftitution: in fuch the filk is always made in larger quantities, and of a far better quality. This is a point which has not been fufficiently attended to, but whenever we come to plant this country, the great advantage of it will be found in making filk.

Cotton is another article which the French cultivated with fuccefs in Louifiana, but which like others never came to be a national object for want of more people, and perhaps for want of encouragement, owing to their fear of rivalling their fugar iflands, which alfo produce it in large quantities. The cotton they cultivated here is a fpecies of the white Siam. This Eaft India and annual cotton has been found to be much better and whiter than what is cultivated in our colonies, which is of the Turkey kind; both of them keep their colour better in wafhing, and are whiter than the perennial cotton that comes from the iflands, although this laft is of a longer ftaple. It is not fo long nor fo foft as the filk-cotton. It is produced, not from a

tree

tree as in the East Indies, but from a plant, and thrives much better in light than in strong and fat land; in the lower lands of Louisiana it never was so fine as on the higher ones. It may be planted on lands newly cleared, and not yet proper for tobacco, much less for indigo, which requires a ground well worked like a garden. The seeds are planted three feet asunder, more or less, according to the quality of the soil; the field is weeded at the proper season, in order to clear it of the noxious weeds, and fresh earth laid to the roots of the plant to secure it against the winds. The cotton requires weeding neither so often nor so carefully as other plants; and the care of gathering is the employment of young people, incapable of harder labour: when the pods burst it is gathered, and the most laborious part of the work is to separate the cotton from the seeds, though it is much lessened since the use of mills was introduced. The high, light, and dry soil in the territory on the east side of the Mississippi is all admirably adapted to this production; and in point of preparation it is not only the fresh that may for the first year be planted with it; after the luxuriance of the soil is abated by tobacco and indigo, it will do exceedingly well for cotton. This article is not mentioned in this or any other case as a proper staple for the sole employment of any colony, but joined with others of greater value, it is a good addition to the best settlements in America; for I have often remarked, what should not be forgotten, that no colony should stick to any one staple so much as to neglect others; the inconveniences of such a conduct are to this day, and have been long felt in our tobacco colonies, where, for want of other staples, such as silk and wine, they have gone too much into common husbandry, which produces nothing wanted in Britain.

The olive tree is common in Louisiana, and very beautiful. The Provençals who were settled here, affirmed that its olives yielded as good an oil as those of their own country. The crop is always very abundant. This is an article which would prove of great advantage to Britain, and of profit to the planters; and no produce would be a staple more proper for a colony. In Carolina, on the coast, the frosts sometimes kill large olive trees; but such extremes of weather are never met with in the high dry territories of this country.

These

These are the principal staples which should be attended to when this country is planted; wine, silk, indigo, tobacco, and cotton; they are valuable commodities, come truly within the definition of a colony *staple*; commodities which this nation either consumes herself, or could command a ready market for; and which are of such value as to enable the planters to purchase negroes in great numbers, so as to enter largely and effectually into their culture. I before shewed that the climate, in respect of health and pleasantness, possessed every advantage that could promote the interests of every branch of agriculture, an object which is of great importance, and in which the British colonies upon the coast, through all that part which is flat and sandy, are greatly deficient. In other respects, the advantages attending this country are equally valuable.

Among these the plenty of wild cattle is not the least, since they not only indicate the fertility of the land, but will afford, for many generations, immense supplies of meat and hides: the principal kinds are deer and buffaloes. All Louisiana contains prodigious tracts, almost boundless they might be called, of rich mea-

meadows, covered with a luxuriant growth of very fine grafs, tracts that have fcarce any interruptions of foreft, hills, or vallies, extend from five to ten and twenty leagues: fuch immenfe paftures of the richeft land, in a warm and fine climate, where the winters yield a plenty of food as well as the fummers, could fcarcely be free from herds of cattle; and accordingly they are found in fuch prodigious numbers, as to aftonifh all travellers that go through the country.

This beaft is about the fize of one of our largeft oxen, but he appears rather bigger on account of his long curled wool, which makes him appear to the eye much larger than he really is. This wool is very fine and very thick. A pretty large bunch rifes on his fhoulders, in the place where they join to the neck. He is the chief food of the natives, and was the fame with the French from the beginning of the colony. The quantity of tallow they yield is very great, and their fkins are an object of no fmall confideration. The natives drefs them with their wool on, as Du Pratz informs us, to fuch great perfection, as to render them more pliable than our buff.

The

The plenty of deer in all parts of this country is very great, notwithstanding the numbers that are constantly killed; they are much the same as the deer of Europe: their skins form one of the most valuable articles of commerce in all the southern colonies of America, and in this country the plenty is yet greater from the immense space of uncultivated land which they have to spread over. Nor is it only in these two articles, which are native to the country, that a great plenty is found; for all the the animals which have been brought from France and the English colonies have multiplied exceedingly; horses, cows, hogs, sheep, &c. are, I apprehend, cheaper than in any of our colonies; this is not to be wondered at, for in no part of America are there found such plenty of natural meadows. The fruits of this country are in the same plenty as Carolina, but of a finer relish from the dryness of the climate; they have besides grapes, plums, papaws, peaches, oranges, citrons, figs, apples, &c. The French colonists planted the peach stones about the end of February, and suffer the trees to grow exposed to all weathers. In the third year they will gather from one tree at least two hundred peaches,

peaches, and double that number for six or seven years more when the tree dies. As new ones are so easily produced, the loss of the old ones is not in the least regretted.

Upon the whole, there is the greatest reason to conclude, that the territory on the east of the Mississippi, which is at present in our possession, is one of the most valuable countries in all America, and one which will pay admirably for colonizing, whenever the measure is thought proper by government to be embraced. It appears on respectable authority, not only of able writers, but gentlemen now living who have travelled through it, that the climate is as fine as any in the world, equally favourable to the production of many valuable staples, and to the health and pleasure of life. That the soil is as fertile as any in the world, though high and dry, circumstances almost invaluable. That the country abounds in an immense plenty of food for cattle, and is spread with vast herds of buffaloes and deer. That fruits, of various kinds, are superior in plenty and flavour to those of any other part of the continent. That indigo, tobacco, hemp, flax, vines, silk, olives, and other

other valuable staples, may be cultivated here with much greater success than in most of the other parts of America. To this if we add the navigation of the Mississippi, and the rivers which fall into it, we shall find the territory to be deficient in no one circumstance that can contribute to render it a flourishing and wealthy colony.

As such, I think there can be no objections rationally made to settling it. The establishment of a new colony on the Ohio might be thought at first sight to supersede it, but if better considered it will not be found so. There is one circumstance in which this territory is much superior to the Ohio, which is that of navigation: the latter has a land carriage across the mountains of forty miles, which will lay a heavy burthen on those commodities that are not very valuable, so as to make it necessary, perhaps, to send them down the Mississippi, in which case the same commodities may be sent to market from this country upon cheaper terms. Nor should we forget to add, that the greater degree of heat on the Mississippi would prove more favourable to several of the staples than the climate of the Ohio, which is not so hot—
and

and we may in general conclude, that the value of the staples of all colonies that are healthy, will be found to increase in proportion to their proximity to the line. This comparison of the two climates concerns only certain articles, for instance, indigo, cotton, and olives, which require for a perfect culture a hotter climate than the Ohio, though indigo may be produced there with profit. But in the case of tobacco, hemp, flax, silk, wine, &c. the Ohio is fully equal; and in all the productions of common husbandry, except Indian corn, perhaps superior. But in another case there is found a strong propriety, at least, in settling the Mississippi, which is the forming a chain of settlements along the banks of that river to the junction with the Ohio colony, in order for strengthening the country on one side against the Spaniards, and on the other against the Indians. The Creeks, Chactaws, Cherokees, and Chicasaws, would then be entirely surrounded, and we should never more have any thing to dread from their resentments: the scheme long ago proposed by several gentlemen of America, well versed in Indian affairs, to stop all supplies of gunpowder for them in case of a war, would

would then be practicable; and without doing them any injury, we should lay the foundation for a perfect security.

In case of such a settlement being made, the whole valuable part of that continent, the southern division of it, would then be in the desirable state of improvement: the population, from being so spread round a great extent of frontier, would increase without giving the least cause of jealousy to Britain, land would not only be plentiful, but plentiful where our people wanted it; whereas at present, the population of our colonies, especially the central ones, is confined; they have spread over all the space between the sea and the mountains, the consequence of which is, that land is become scarce, that which is good having been all planted or patented, the people therefore find themselves too numerous for their agriculture, which is the first step to be manufactures, that step which Britain has so much reason to dread. Nothing therefore can be more political, than to provide a superabundance of colonies to take off all those people that find a want of land in our old settlements; and it may not be one or two tracts of country that will answer this purpose; provision should be be made for the convenience of some, the inclinations of others, and every measure taken to inform the people of the colonies that were growing too populous, that land was plentiful in other places, and granted on the easiest terms; and if such inducements were not found sufficient for thinning the country considerably, government should, by all means, be at a part of the expence of transporting them. Notice should be given that sloops should always be ready at Fort Pit, or as much higher on the Ohio as it is navigable; for carrying all families, without expence, to whatever settlements they chuse on the Ohio or the Mississippi. Such measures, or similar ones, would carry off that surplus of population in the central and northern colonies, which has been, and will every day be more and more the foundation of their manufactures. They never could establish such fabrics, while the plenty of good land in a good climate was so great as to afford every man an opportunity of settling; for while that was the case, none would let themselves as workmen in a manufacture. Consistent with these ideas, we see that those colonies where the good land is most plentiful in a good climate, the manufactures are

are trifling, or none to be found, which is the case with the tobacco colonies and with the southern ones; but in the northern settlements, where these circumstances are different, we there find many fabrics.

Nothing can be more fortunate than the navigation of the Ohio quite to the Apalachean mountains, at the back of the center of all our colonies, since by that means people may, with only a small or a moderate journey, arrive at a navigation that will carry them through all that immense tract which we may in future colonize, a part of which we are now about to settle, and yet more of which I am urging the propriety of likewise settling. Were it not for this vast navigation, to the very spot almost that one would wish to have it, there would be difficulties in the people getting to the countries we wanted them to settle in; but as we possess this great advantage, it would be unpardonable not to make effectual use of it, in case the establishment of new colonies did not of itself draw the whole surplus of population away from those provinces, the numbers in which want so much to be thinned.

Nor is the advantage of drawing off people from the northern colonies confined

to

to the prevention of manufactures; it is further of vast consequence to take them from countries that produce nothing valuable in a British market, and fix them in others abounding with staples of high importance to the commerce and manufactures of the mother-country: this single idea ought to be the corner-stone of all the regulations and measures adopted by this country in her transactions with America; and if it is well pursued in future, will keep off the dangerous rivalship, which there is so much reason to fear, from the manufactures and commerce of the northern colonies.

If the country on the east bank of the Mississippi was settled, and that to the south of the Ohio also, there would be such a variety of land, climate, and productions, that every new comer, either from Europe or our own colonies, would have it in his power to chuse the culture with which he was best acquainted, or by which he expected to make the most considerable profits: they might fix on the climate most agreeable to their constitutions, and in all other respects have such a variety of circumstances to select from, that the temptation to move would be very great.

great. At the same time that they suited themselves, they could not fail, fix where they would, of promoting the interest of the mother-country in a very sensible degree. By not delaying such a measure, there would be a population, and with it a power fixed in the most important part of all this continent, upon this immense inland navigation, which spreads far and near, from the Atlantic Ocean to the South Sea, and from the Gulph of Mexico to Hudson's Bay: the river Mississippi with its branches spread over most of it, and the lakes, with the St. Laurence, which are nearly connected with the former, go through the rest. It is of prodigious future consequence to be masters of this navigation, and to have early a power fixed on it, in order to over-awe and keep the Spaniards from designs against our colonies. We ought not to forget their jealousy of us in this country, and that they have at present a much greater military force there than ever was possessed by the French. It is a mistake to imagine that the Spaniards have been inattentive to the *security* of their American colonies; as backward as they have always been in their improvement, they have been far enough from negligence with relation to a military power, I mean since the last peace, for upon the conclusion of it, their whole army was dispatched from Old to New Spain, and the arrangement of the former left entirely to new levies. This was a very bold and decisive measure, and which shewed a resolution to be stronger in America than ever was experienced before: it is for this reason that we ought to be particularly attentive to the strength of our territories on the Missisippi, and to give them it effectually must be done by peopling them, instead of keeping the whole country in as desolate a condition as it was a century before the French discovered it.

General O'Reilly, when he took possession of New Orleans, had a force of five thousand regular troops, with a good train of artillery, and every requisite for a small but well appointed army. This force they have maintained here; it is much superior to any thing we have in West Florida and upon the Missisippi; our government therefore ought certainly to be upon their guard in this part of the world, and not only to have a sufficient military force in the forts and armed sloops upon the river, but a chain of populous settlements to cut off all possibility of communication between the Spaniards and the Indians to the east of the Missisippi; a point which may in future prove of very great consequence.

CHAP.

CHAP. XXVIII.

THE ILIONOIS.

Country of the Ilionois — Climate — Soil — Productions — Importance of this territory — Observations.

BY the country of the Ilionois, I mean all that territory to the north-west of the Ohio, extending on both sides the river Ilionois quite to Lake Michigan and the river St. Joseph, the settlements made by the French on the river Myamis; but in particular the country east of the Mississippi, between the Ohio and Ilionois river, to the distance of about an hundred miles from the former. This territory went among the French by the general name of the country of the Ilionois. It claims attention in this work, first because we are in possession of all the settlements made by the French in it, and notwithstanding its being deficient in all government but that of the commanding officers of our forts, they have increased considerably by the wandering settlers from our colonies:

colonies: and secondly, because the great richness of the soil and fertility of the climate will hereafter attract so many inhabitants, as to make the establishment of some civil government highly necessary. The public accounts given of this country are not numerous, but what there are, are very consistent with each other, and also with the private information I have received from the officers with whom I have conversed, that made a considerable residence here.

Charlevoix, who passed through this country, has given some slight descriptions of different parts, which will afford a pretty good idea of it: he entered it by Lake Erie, the country upon which though not included in it, yet is so near as to deserve our attention here. Of the tract on the very southern point of that lake, he speaks as follows. " I coasted along a charming country, hid at times by very disagreeable prospects, which however are of no great extent. Wherever I went ashore, I was quite enchanted by the beauty and variety of a landscape, which was terminated by the noblest forests in the whole world. Add to this that every part of it swarms with water-fowl; I cannot say whether

whether the woods afford game in equal profusion; but I well know that there is a prodigious quantity of buffaloes. Were we always to fail, as I then did, with a serene sky, in a most charming climate, and on water as clear as that of the purest fountain; were we sure of finding every where secure and agreeable places to pass the night in, where we might enjoy the pleasure of hunting at a small expence, breathe at our ease the purest air, and enjoy the prospect of the finest countries in the universe, we might possibly be tempted to travel to the end of our days."

Of the country between Lakes Erie and Huron, he says, "It is pretended that this is the finest part of all Canada; and really, if we may judge by appearances, nature seems to have refused it nothing that can contribute to make a country delightful; hills, meadows, fields, lofty forests, rivulets, fountains, rivers, and all of them so excellent in their kind, and so happily blended, as to equal the most romantic wishes; the lands, however, are not all equally proper for every sort of grain, but most are of a wonderful fertility, and I have known some produce good wheat for eighteen years running, without any manure

manure; and besides, all of them are proper for some particular use. The islands in the channel, between the two lakes, seemed placed on purpose for the pleasure of the prospect; the river and lake abound in fish, the air is pure, and the climate temperate and extremely wholesome. There grow here citron trees in the open fields, the fruit of which, in shape and colour, resemble those of Portugal, but they are smaller and of a disagreeable flavour. On both sides of the channel the country is said to preserve its beauty for ten leagues up; after which you meet with a smaller number of fruit trees and fewer meadows; but after travelling five or six leagues further, inclining to Lake Erie towards the south-west, you discover immense meadows, extending above a hundred leagues every where, and which feed an immense quantity of those buffaloes, whereof I have more than once made mention. Twelve leagues off this channel, before you come to Lake Huron, is a village of Missisaguy Indians, seated on a fertile soil, at the entry of three magnificent meadows, and in the most most charming situation that can be, the country for the whole twelve leagues continuing always most delightful.

This

This is a noble channel, as strait as a line, and bordered with lofty forests, interspersed with fine meadows, with many islands scattered up and down in it, some of which are considerably large."

Of the territory on the river St. Joseph, he speaks as follows. " The river St. Joseph has more than an hundred leagues of course, its source being at no great distance from Lake Erie; it is navigable for fourscore leagues, and as I was sailing up towards the fort, I saw nothing but excellent lands, covered with trees of a prodigious height. Tobacco grows well here, and by making a proper choice of soil, we might raise a most excellent sort of it."

Proceeding to the south by the river Huakiki, which falls into the Ilionois, he observes, that " at about fifty leagues from the source the country becomes beautiful, consisting of unbounded meadows, where buffaloes are to be seen grazing in herds of two or three hundred. Where the Huakiki joins the Ilionois, the latter becomes a fine river; it does not yield in largeness to any of our rivers in France, and I can assure you, it is not possible to behold a finer and a better country than this which it waters. Before we came to Lake Pimiteouy

teouy, we crossed a charming country, and at the end of that lake came to a village of the Ilionois; than which nothing can be more delightful than its situation: opposite to it is the prospect of a most beautiful forest, which was then adorned with all the variety of colours, and behind it is a plain of an immense extent, skirted with woods. The lake and river swarm with fish, and the banks of both with game. From the lake to the Mississippi the river Ilionois, both in breadth and depth, is equal to any of the greatest rivers of Europe. After sailing five leagues on the Mississippi, we arrived at the mouth of the Missouri. Here is the finest confluence of two rivers that I believe is to be met with in the whole world, each of them being about half a league in breadth; but the Missouri is by far the most rapid of the two, and seems to enter the Mississippi like a conqueror, carrying its white waters, unmixed, across its channel quite to the opposite side; this colour it afterwards communicates to the Mississippi, which henceforth it never loses, but hurls with precipitation to the sea itself."

About Fort Chartres the French have several settlements, and live pretty much at

at their ease: they sow wheat, which succeeds very well; and they have black cattle and poultry. The banks of the river are extremely high, so that though the waters sometimes rise five and twenty feet, they seldom overflow their channel. All this country is open, consisting of vast meadows, to the extent of five and twenty leagues, which are intersperfed with small copses of very valuable wood. White mulberries especially are very common here; but I am surprised that the inhabitants should be suffered to cut them down for the building of their houses, especially as there is a sufficient quantity of other trees equally proper for that purpose. The whole country, from hence to Kascasquias, and around the latter, is very fertile; it is capable of becoming the grainery of Louisiana, which it is able to furnish with corn in abundance, even should it be peopled quite to the sea. The soil is not only extremely proper for wheat, but besides, refuses nothing necessary or useful for human life. The climate is extremely temperate, lying in 38 deg. 39 min. north lat. Cattle and sheep would multiply here wonderfully, even the wild buffaloes might be tamed, and great advantages drawn from
a trade

a trade of their wool and hides, and from their supplying the inhabitants with food. The air is very wholesome. Frosts are sometimes felt that are very severe; the river last winter was frozen over in such a manner, that people crossed it in carriages, notwithstanding it is at that place half a league broad, and more rapid than the Rhone. This is the more surprising, as for the most part, excepting a few slight frosts occasioned by the north and north-west winds, the winter is in this country hardly sensible; the leaves fall sooner in this place than in France, and do not begin to bud till about the end of May, notwithstanding that it snows very seldom here, and although, as I have already observed, the winters are exceeding temperate. What then can be the reason of this backwardness of the spring? for my part I can see no other than the thickness of the forests, which prevents the earth from being warmed by the sun soon enough to cause the sap to ascend. At Cape St. Anthony I saw the first canes."

I have been led to make these long extracts from Charlevoix, because his authority has always been justly esteemed, and he gave this account long before the country

try became subject to Britain: although he only touches upon certain circumstances of the soil and climate, as a traveller and not a resident, yet may we gather from it that both are excellent, that the soil is fertile in yielding tobacco and the articles of common husbandry, particularly wheat; that the forests are among the finest in the world; the meadows of an unbounded extent, and full of buffaloes; that the air is pure and healthy, and the climate in every respect temperate and agreeable; and lastly, that the beauty of many tracts of this country is as great as the finest assemblage of wood, water, hill, and dale can make it.

Much later accounts confirm these particulars. When Charlevoix was there, in 1721, the French had but begun to cultivate it, but since that period they have made a great progress; so that at the peace of 1762 they had a fine and well settled colony about Kascasquias and Fort Chartres, and also many settlements on the river Myamis, principally inhabited by emigrants from Canada: some of these sold their effects, and retired upon the conclusion of the peace, but the major part remained under the British government; nor has the country declined since, notwithstanding

standing the only government established in it is that of the commanding officers of the garrisoned forts.

Mr. Pownal, in his *Administration of the Colonies*, gives, from very good authority, a few particulars concerning the country of the Ilionois. " This country, says Charlevoix, in 1721 will become the grainery of Louisiana; and in 1746 we find it actually becoming so, for in that year it sent down to New Orleans fifty ton of flour; in 1747 we find it well furnished with provisions, and having fine crops; and in a letter of Monf. Vandreuil's, in 1748, we have an account of its produce and exports—flour, corn, bacon, hams both of bears and hogs, corned pork, and wild beef, myrtle-wax, cotton, tallow, leather, tobacco, lead, copper, some small quantity of buffalo wool, venison, poultry, bear's grease, oil, skins, and some coarse furs; and we find a regular communication settled with New Orleans, by convoys, which come down annually the latter end of December, and return at latest by the middle of February."

The private accounts I have had of this country confirm the preceding articles of intelligence, and give the greatest reason for

for determining that it ranks among the best and most agreeable of America; especially in every circumstance that concerns the plenty and agreeableness of living, and all the productions of common husbandry, in which I believe it yields to no part of the world. As to staples in a British market, it will be by no means deficient in them, whenever the advantages of the climate are any ways seconded in these respects by the skill and industry of the planters. Tobacco may undoubtedly be produced here in any quantity, and of a quality equal to any other: the country, most of it, in the same latitude as Virginia and Maryland, with the advantage of a much more regular climate, and winters less severe. Charlevoix expressly says, that in general the winters are exceedingly temperate; whereas in Virginia extreme sharp frosts are common: but through all our southern and central colonies the maritime parts are exposed to greater degrees of heat and cold than the internal country. The navigation of the Mississippi will make the culture of tobacco very profitable. Wine may also be a most beneficial staple to this country, the climate is perfectly agreeable to it, and high, dry, and hilly tracts common throughout the whole territory: the navigation will be equally favourable to the product of this country. Silk is another which will undoubtedly be made in confiderable quantities whenever the territory is peopled, fince the healthinefs and temperature of the climate cannot in this latitude but agree admirably with the worm, and mulberries are plentifully fpread over the whole of it. In a word, it is deficient in no article that can tend to render it a valuable colony, and whenever it is fettled will be found of that importance to this kingdom, of which we have already experienced thofe to be that poffefs ftaple productions.

CHAP.

CHAP. XXIX.

JAMAICA.

Climate — Soil — Productions — The culture of Sugar — Expences — Produce — Profit — Observations — Other staples — Settlements — Remarkable instances of beneficial improvements — Observations.

THE amazing importance which has attended the culture of the sugar cane, is perhaps one of the most extraordinary instances of the effect of agriculture that the world has produced, and it shews clearer than any other circumstance wherein consists the true and beneficial nature of colonies: the profit which this nation reaps from her islands in the West Indies ought above all other things to make her attentive to every particular in the culture of the sugar cane. As Jamaica is our principal colony for this production, I shall be more minute in my account than in the description of other islands, as they will call only for the circumstances wherein they differ from that island.

Jamaica lies between 17 and 19 deg. north latitude, from whence it is easy to judge that the climate is extremely hot: indeed the sun passes directly over their heads, and would, in the height of summer, render the air too suffocating to breathe, were it not for the trade wind and land breeze which refresh and cool the air. Yet with this advantage which Jamaica enjoys in common with the rest of the islands, the climate is in general pernicious to European constitutions. The extreme heat is not so great an enemy as the dampness and moisture which attend it: and we may in general remark, that this is the circumstance which in all latitudes, but especially hot ones, decides the healthiness of a country. A dry and pure air, such as is found on hilly or mountainous sea-coasts, free from marshes or swamps, is always healthy, though under the line; but when a meridian sun unites with a marshy rotten soil, in which the heavy rains stagnate, then it is impossible for a country to be tolerably healthy. The people of Jamaica lament their thunders and lightnings, their tempests and hurricanes—the last are indeed very fatal to their profit; but if health was only considered, a low marshy tract of of land, in parts of which the rains stagnated, should be considered as a much more fatal circumstance. The great evil of the climate is its moisture, which, united with heat, brings that numerous list of fatal distempers which are common in this island; which renders caution in diet and living remarkably necessary, and which is worse than fatal in causing that extreme languor of the body and oppression of the spirits, which make the inhabitants suffer worse than death through half their existence. In a word, the climate of Jamaica is such an one, as nothing but the hope of wealth could induce an Englishman to live in. With an exception, however, of the hilly tracts, which, and the mountains, are by no means unhealthy for a hot climate.

The island is entirely out of the reach of frost and snow, nor have they ever any weather that can be denominated cold: they have properly neither winter nor summer, for the trees never lose their leaves; the only distinction of season is that of the rains, which fall in July, August, and September, but principally in August. They have also heavy ones in May and October, and sometimes a season (that is a rain) happens in January. Their hurricanes are extremely dreadful; in some of them the wind is so furious, and rises to such a pitch in a few minutes, that every obstacle flies before it; trees of an immense size are torn up by the roots, and blown away like chaff—whole groves disappear in an instant—buildings, however solidly constructed of stone, and the walls, many feet thick, purposely constructed to withstand these terrible blasts, are destroyed in a moment; in a word, the surface of the earth is truly bared, every thing is swept from it with irresistible violence: it may easily be imagined, that, in such a situation, the canes and other objects of culture are the first to be blown away. These storms of wind are not all of equal violence, nor do they spread a large tract of country at once; buildings very strongly built sometimes escape, at others every thing gives way.

Jamaica is about one hundred and forty miles long by sixty broad, and contains about four millions of acres. But much the greater part is not patented to any owners, and a very small portion of it is cultivated. The face of the country is extremely various. Along the middle of the island, from east to west, runs a vast chain of mountains, called the Blue Mountains: these occupy above half the island, for they spread in various ridges, some higher

higher than others, with deep furrowed glens between them; and in some places flat vales of amazing fertility are found, quite surrounded with rock and precipice. The hills are all either rock or stiff tenacious clay; every thing else is washed down into the vales by torrents, cascades, and waterfalls, which are numerous, or by the heavy rains in general; thus all the lower lands are found to be a loose friable mould, prodigiously fertile—as the want of roads and navigation prevent their being cultivated, they are generally covered with fine grass, but some are forest. Most of the hills and even the rocks, though apparently without earth, are covered with large and strait timber trees of various sorts: so that nothing can be seen more romantic or noble to behold than the mountainous scenes, which are usually formed of a great intermixture of rocks, mountains, woods, and waterfalls, with gleams of vale of the finest verdure. The country from the sea-coast to the hills is various, but generally consists of woods, marshes, swamps, savannahs, or meadows, and cultivated plantations; many tracts are sandy, but there are none but what produce some article or other spontaneously, which adds to the wealth of the owners, except indeed some of the undrained swamps, which are totally useless.

Among the productions of this island we may reckon sugar, cocoa, indigo, pimento, wild cinnamon, coffee, cotton, tobacco, fustic, red wood, logwood, guaiacum, china root, sarsaparilla, cassia, tamarinds, venilloes, cochineal, mahogany, manchineal, &c. Among these articles, what chiefly claims our notice at present, is the culture of sugar.

The sugar cane is a reed, smooth and jointed, of a shining, greenish, yellow colour. Their size varies according to soil, culture, &c. but the height is generally from four to eight feet, but in some soils they do not rise above two or three feet; in others we sometimes see them nine, ten, or more. In the French islands we are told by Labat, that canes have been known four and twenty feet in length, exclusive of the top and lower joint, and each weighed twenty-four pounds. The largest canes are three or four inches thick, but generally not above an inch.

They are propagated by cuttings; pieces from fifteen to eighteen inches long are cut from the tops of the canes, a little below

low the upper leaves: the more knots or eyes there are, the better. The season of planting is principally August, being the height of the rainy season; but it is a work which is done also in September and October, and even quite to January and February, but not later. Before we proceed with the culture, I shall describe the soils usually chosen for a plantation.

In Jamaica the best soil for sugar is the red brick earth, strong, but not clayey; black mould on clay is excellent; all loose friable lands, not very sandy, will do very well, and are of a value proportioned to their moisture; drained swamps, marshes, and bogs, from which the water is carried clean off, frequently do well. But let me in general remark, that a sugar planter's choice of soil is very similar to that of a good English farmer; so that good land is the same in all countries; the mere stiff clay is not good with either; but all loams are excellent; brushy wet gravels are rejected by both; light sands in a hot climate are worse than in England; black mould is every where excellent; and drained bogs and marshes, wherever found, are generally fertile: thus is there not that mystery in judging of soils in different climates that many would persuade us. Poorer lands in Jamaica,

maica, as well as in England, require the assistance of dunging and other manuring, and the best yield crops proportioned to such management. The richest soils are fresh woodlands, which when cleared from the wood, and much of the rubbish burnt upon the land, prove for many years an inexhaustible fund of fertility and wealth to the planter; but those woodlands in Jamaica, which are near enough to water-carriage, are mostly taken up and cleared, for if this requisite is wanting, the richest soils will not pay for culture.

Respecting the preparation of the ground, it is brought into tillage and rendered clear of weeds; the former is effected by hand-hoeing, and is repeated till the weeds are all destroyed: the worst is the *withe*, which like couch grass in England has such a vegetative property, that the least bit left in the ground grows and multiplies very fast; it climbs up and strangles the canes. The roots of trees must also be destroyed if they are of a kind that sends up suckers or shoots; this is done by burning or scorching them: but other roots they are not attentive to destroy, for as the tillage is given with hoes, it is not necessary to extract such obstructions as would stop the plough. If the land to be planted is fresh, or in great heart, they do not manure, but if it has been long under canes, or out of order, ample manuring is neceffary. In raifing dung, they rank among the beft farmers in the world, and this I take to be owing to the difficulty of procuring it; in England, where the winters enable good hufbandmen to raife almoft any quantity they pleafe, it is much neglected; but in Jamaica, where they have no winter, and where the heat of the fun is in general a great hindrance to the work, they are forced to be indefatigable in the work, or they would never effect it.

The refufe of the fugar canes affifts them as litter and food for the cattle; the cane tops and leaves of Guinea corn are given the cattle plentifully in pens, where they wafte enough to make litter; the pen is firft fpread thickly with marle or earth, generally the former, and by feeding many horfes, affes, mules, cows, oxen, and fwine in them, by their dung and urine and wafte of food they add a layer upon the marle; and prodigioufly enrich the whole compoft. Then more marle is carted in, and the cattle fed upon that in the fame manner; and fo in fucceffion till it is wanted for the plantation, when the cattle are moved into other pens, and the compost is turned over and mixed well together, after which it will in a little time be ready for carrying out. This management of cattle lasts through the whole year.

I must observe upon it, that it is a system which deserves universal imitation in all countries, how far feeding fat cattle in pens would do in summer is not clear, but as to all lean stock, such as draught oxen, horses, cows, young cattle, swine, &c. it would beyond all doubt answer extremely well: marle, chalk, clay, turf, or earth, should, as in Jamaica, be carted into the farm yards and spread in an even layer about them; upon this should be all the foddering which the farmers bestow upon their cattle; and in summer the system should be continued, by feeding them with grass or clover, &c. mown and given fresh in racks; upon this plan their food would go infinitely farther than in the common way, and they would make four times the quantity of dung they do at present. Necessity obliges the planters in Jamaica to pursue a method, which, if the farmers of Britain would pursue, they would certainly find the same great advantages from.

When

When the plantations are upon a clay or a stiff soil, they mix sand with the compost, by carrying it in and forming a layer in the pens in the same manner as marle; and the good effects have been often experienced. Ashes of all burnt vegetables are used with care, and their effects said to be great.

After the field has been sufficiently prepared it is marked out, and holes made in regular rows to receive the dung, upon which the canes are planted. This work is called *holing:* the methods used are not all the same, nor the distances. Some make the holes four or five feet asunder, or four by five, and put two or three sets in a hole; but the most common method is to make trenches from four to eight inches deep, according to the weather, in which they lay the canes, and cover them; these trenches are sometimes laid out by lines, and ought always to be. The distance between the rows and betwixt the plants in each row may in good ground be about three feet and a half; in poor worn-out grounds two feet are sufficient.

But let it here be remarked, that this way of regularly disposing of the canes is only followed by the best planters; there are more that plant promiscuously, but it is a very erroneous

erroneous method, which ought to be exploded. The land planted in either case is in squares, formed by intervals fifteen feet wide, which cross the field at right angles, and are of great use in several instances; they admit carts to be loaded in harvest with the canes, without going over the ploughed ground, which is very mischievous to the crop; and they prevent the spreading of fires, made on purpose to burn trash, or accidental ones; they give a free path to the planter to view the state of the canes, and the negroes when employed in hoeing them; nor is the land occupied by such intervals lost, as pease, beans, potatoes, and other plants may be cultivated in them, that come off before the sugar canes are cut.

When the canes are about eighteen inches high, which will be in a fortnight or three weeks after planting, they are cleared from weeds, and the soil about them loosened by hand-hoeing; and this operation is repeated two or three times, as it happens, till the plants are arrived at such a growth and thickness as to kill all weeds by their thick shade.

The canes are cut when in full maturity, which in dry loose soils is generally at the end

end of fourteen or fifteen months after being planted; but in cold clay soils not till sixteen or seventeen months. They are cut with hand-bills, as close to the ground as possible, then cleared from their leaves, &c. and cut into shorter pieces, from two feet and a half to four feet in length. The chief precaution here is, that the cane be cut off smooth, without hacking the root, which in the dry season is of great prejudice to it. The top of the cane, to the distance of three or four inches below the flag, should be cut off along with the leaves: some are accustomed to save this part, and endeavour to turn the whole of the cane to advantage; but this is a piece of ill-judged frugality: the top of the cane is always green, and contains only a crude, unripe juice, which, mingling with the rest, will greatly debase it.

On cutting the canes they are immediately carried to the mill, usually a windmill, in which being ground between iron cylinders, the juice is pressed out, and flows through a tube into a vat; thence it is conducted through a pipe into another vat, and after that to the cauldron in the boiling house; it is then boiled, and as fast as any scum arises it is taken off; it runs from this boiler through four or five more, smaller and smaller, in all which it is likewise boiled till it becomes a thick glutinous consistence: when boiling can be carried on no farther, a fermentation is raised by lime water, which is subsided by a small piece of butter, after which it is taken into coolers, where it dries and granulates. In this operation of boiling, the fires are kept in night and day, and the boilers filled in succession, as fast as empty, with fresh juice; the fewel is dried cane trash stacked ready for use, and faggots cut from copses planted on purpose, or from logwood hedges, which are of a very quick growth.

After the sugar is dried and grannulated, it is put into pots of a sugarloaf form, open at the point, through which aperture the dregs of the sugar falls; these dregs are melasses, or treacle, when it has sufficiently purified itself, it is called muscovado sugar, being then in order to be put into the hogshead and shipped off. Some planters chusing to refine it yet farther, cover the sugar in the pots with white tobacco-pipe clay kneaded with water, which, sinking through the sugar, carries down more of the melasses than will go off without it, leaving the sugar much whiter than the

musco-

muscovado: and at the discretion of the planter the work is repeated once or twice more, the quality each time increasing in value, but the quantity diminishing. After this operation it is called *clayed* sugar.

From the melasses rum is distilled, by means of fermentation in the common method of gaining all other spirits; they gain in this island from a puncheon to 65 hogsheads of rum to every hogshead of sugar, but much of their melasses are sold to New England to be distilled there.

In the continuation of the culture it is to be observed, that after the canes are cut the land is hoed quite clean, and miscarriages among the canes replanted: the shoots that are sent forth by the stools are called rattoons, which in due time yield a second crop nearly as luxuriant as the first, but not always so, the management of which is exactly the same as of the first crop. The duration of the plants, however, depends upon the soil; in poor or worn out ones they will have only one rattoon crop, but but in very rich and fresh soils they cut several. Labat says, that in some of the French islands they will continue yielding for fifteen or twenty years; but no such thing happens generally.

Upon

Upon the system of cutting a crop but twice the planters divide their cane land into three parts. One is fallow, prepared either with the plough or the hoe for planting; the second is the crop in its first year; the third is the crop in its second year. By this means a third is planted new, and two thirds cut in every period of the growth of the crop; that part which this year (of fifteen or sixteen months) is fallow, next year is the crop of the first growth; that part which this year is the crop of the first growth will next year be the rattoon crop; and that part which this year is the rattoon crop, will next year be fallow. Cane grounds are in general from ten to twenty-five acres each piece. The whole system is transferred continually from old ground to new, according to circumstances.

The buildings upon a plantation are very considerable and expensive; they consist principally of a mansion-house, windmill, boiling-house, furnaces, store-houses, sheds, &c. the furniture of which, such as cylinders, vats, coppers, pipes, tubes, reservoirs, coolers, &c. are costly.

Before I give any account of the expences and profit of the culture, I shall make some observations on the essential faults with which

which their agriculture in this article abounds. First, the preparation of the ground, which is generally fallowed with hoes; though ploughs are used by a few planters, yet the number is inconsiderable. In clearing a piece of fresh ground, they destroy the wood in the manner practised in the colonies, that is, saw it off and leave the stump to rot in the ground: this effectually precludes the plough. The hoeing culture is more trivial than can easily be credited; for in strength and efficacy it is not comparable to the same operation given by the farmers in England to several crops. Three, four, or five hundred negroes have been seen hoeing a piece of forty acres; they cut about an inch deep, sometimes if the soil is loose a little deeper, and at others not half an inch; if the planter attains any depth that approaches that of ploughing, the expence he is at to get it is enormous. Now it should not be forgotten, that the cane roots at a depth proportioned to the loosened mould upon soils that have any tenacity, indeed in very friable sandy loams, or loose hazle mould, the roots strike much deeper than the hoe has been, or they would not thrive at all; and to remedy these evils it is that holing is practised, in which

which they dig small holes where the canes are to be set, to receive the dung and cane set: but such methods in every article of husbandry throughout the world are bad: the roots of all crops should be encouraged to spread over the whole land, instead of being confined to spots where the dung is put, which is always the consequence of not dunging the whole land. Then comes the planting, in which the planters exclude every thing but the hand-hoe, by setting the canes promiscuously; those that plant in rows, use no other tool; the consequence of which is, that the keeping the spaces between the plants loose, in good order, and free from weeds, is all performed by the negroes with their hand-hoes, which is just such management as to use no other tool between the rows of a field of cabbages in England, planted wide enough to admit of horse-hoeing; which in this country would be an expence of ten or twelve shillings for very badly performing an operation, which might be very well done for half a crown.

The two errors I have here disclosed are very essential ones, and in the conduct of them render such prodigious stocks of negroes necessary, as eat amazingly into the
profit

profit of the planter. Hence therefore arises the necessity of pointing out methods whereby they may escape such expences, and at the same time execute their work in a much superior manner.

In the preparation of my ground, I would carry the ideas of the improved husbandry of England into that of sugar in Jamaica; I would, in clearing my fresh land, remove all obstacles which might stop the plough, such as roots or large stones; this expence would be well repaid by my successive advantages. I would then plough the fallow of a depth proportioned to that of the soil; in rich deep lands I would go a foot, but in shallower soils eight inches: before the last ploughing I would spread the dung or compost all over the land; and immediately turn it in by the last ploughing, leaving the surface, when the work was completed, flat on dry soils, and ridged on wet ones.

In the next place, my ploughman should draw furrows by the eye, as strait as an arrow, at the distance of three, four, or five feet, according to the distance of the rows of canes, which should be regulated by the fertility of the soil: the richer the land the greater the distance. In these furrows I would

I would lay the cane sets, and cover them by drawing mould over them by negroes with hand-hoes: let us suppose the rows equally distant four feet asunder. As soon as the plants were a foot high, I would run a Berkshire shim, the cutting plate three feet wide, through the intervals; it should cut about two inches deep, in order to cut down the weeds, and loosen the surface of the land: at the same time the rows should be hand-weeded. But if the soil was stoney, instead of the Berkshire, the Kentish shim should be used, which has three triangular shares instead of one flat one in the other.

These operations should be repeated often enough to keep the soil loose: when the plants were come to that point of growth that made earthing proper, I would run a double-winged plough, the mould-board of which extends or contracts at pleasure, through each interval, the wings so extended as just to throw a surge of mould along the roots of the plants. Such a plough will perform that work better than any hand-hoe; and by thus earthing once or twice, after other operations of horse-hoeing, the well tilled earth of the intervals, after being well mixed and intimately united

united with the dung, would be thrown to the roots to supply them with nourishment as their growth demanded it.

After a trench was thus opened in the middle of each interval, I should go in with shims that took a narrower cut, in order to keep pulverizing the interval till the growth of the canes shut out the horses. After the crop was cut in the usual manner, another great advantage would arise; by laying them in bundles on the top of every third or fourth ridge, carts constructed so as the wheels should spread eight feet, and go each in a trench with the horses in that between them, the carts would be admitted to every part of the plantation without doing the least injury to the stools or roots of the cane: it is upon this system that farmers in England carry cabbages, &c. from off wet lands in winter without poaching. Another benefit arising from this mode of culture, would be the following operation. After the plantation was cleared, I should widen the wings of the double plough, and passing it through every interval, throw a ridge of mould over the cane stools, covering them up, which with such an implement is very easily performed, and very completely in the effect: this practice, performed with hoes at a great expence, has in several of our islands been found excellent; consequently this compendious way would do it in a manner much superior, and at a twentieth of the expence.

If any considerate person reflects upon this system, in comparison of the method of hand-work now in use, which is certainly the most expensive conduct that is known in any part of the world—he will, I am confident, allow that the saving of expence would be prodigious, and the culture at the same time performed in a manner far superior. The objections that will be made to it (for what plan was ever thought of, against which objections could not be started?) I can easily suppose may be numerous. Those which I have heard, that carry any appearance of reason with them, are the following.

First, that the number of mules, &c. which would be necessary, could not be kept without a greater expence than the present number of negroes. I must be allowed to deny this, as a circumstance perfectly incredible: let it be remembered, that most of the planters are obliged to keep very large herds of cattle merely for the purpose of making dung, why not therefore let a larger proportion of them be draught cattle for the purpose of tillage? A well-fed beast that works will make as good dung as a beast that does not work; but granting that a larger stock of cattle would be necessary, the quantity of dung raised would be proportioned, and that advantage, where dung is so valuable, would go far to pay the extra expence. But why not appropriate a larger part of the estate to the production of food for cattle? I do not apprehend there is any part of the world in which cattle pays so well, and the want of food is rather owing to the negligence of the cultivator than denied by the climate. Cane tops at one season afford the most luxuriant supply in the world —and stacks of them are made by way of hay, which yield a plenty through some months: the leaves of Indian corn are also made the same use of, and found of high advantage: but the returns made in Jamaica by Scotch grass, as they commonly call it, the greater panic grass, is prodigious. The quantity of its produce exceeds that of any other fodder whatsoever, and yields in value a produce to the amount sometimes of fifty or sixty pounds an acre.

When

When such ample products are to be had, with the assistance in many parts of Jamaica of large savannahs or meadows, and barley, pease, and beans imported from North America at a very moderate price, it must surely be evident enough, that any quantity of cattle might be kept for the advantageous purpose of substituting horse or mule tillage for that of hand-work—and the profit attending the practice would certainly be immense.

But let us suppose the expence attending cattle greater than it really is, are we to be allowed nothing in the saving of negroes, that most expensive mode of labour? Two mules or oxen and one man with a shim will do more work in a day than twenty good negroes; but who will be so hardy as to assert, that the former can possibly cost the planter as much as the latter: in the earthing up the plants three mules or oxen, a double mould-board plough, and two men, will do more work than thirty-five negroes. In the preparation of the field a plough, two, three, or four mules, and one or two men will, supposing the depth of tillage the same, perform more work than an hundred negroes; but they will not be able to go the depth at all, and therefore the superiority

ority is the greater: if a less depth is stirred, the plough, or a wide shim of four feet, would do a proportionate quantity of land. Now can any persons be so senseless or prejudiced, as to suppose that the saving in negroes would not infinitely more than pay for the increase of expence in cattle?

Secondly, it is objected that the nature of the climate is such as will not admit of the tillage and horse-hoeing I have recommended; that the rains are so amazingly impetuous, and the successive sun-shine so powerful, as to bind many soils into a hard cement, which could not be wrought by the tools I have described: but in answer to this, I appeal to the common sense of every understanding person, whether horse-work will not prove more effectual than the weak exertion of the negroes hoes? The harder the soil is bound, the less able are they to make an impression on it: if the land was like a baked hard trodden path, the hoes would be useless; but no turnpike road in England is too hard to be torn in pieces by horse-work. But the assertion is not true; cane grounds so hard as to be difficultly worked by horse-hoes, would be in such order as none but a sloven could bear; the crop would be nothing; it is a plant that requires as loose friable a soil as any other, and always in that condition: stiff soils must be rendered open with much dung and compost; and a soil that is well manured can never bind in any climate. As to such degrees of baking as really happen, small variations in the horse-hoeing would answer: I would, for instance, be provided with a scarificator or plough of coulters alone to spread two or three feet of ground, and cut it into stripes, which would destroy all that caking of the surface which the objection supposes, and which would prepare it for the other operations I have proposed. Another tool proper to be provided with is a spiky roller, weighing several tons, about eight feet long, for working the fallow; and also a small globular one to work in the trenches of the intervals between the rows of canes; these three instruments would effectually answer all such objections as this.

Thirdly, it is answered, that the distances of the rows necessary for the admission of the horse-hoes I have described would be too great for the production of a full crop of canes;—I am sensible that the majority of planters set their canes in the promiscuous method, at nearer distances than

than I have supposed; but let me observe, that supposing such practice judicious and necessary, yet is it no objection to my system, since I could horse-hoe wherever the negroes could hand-hoe. English farmers, upon much the same principles, assert, that four or five bushels of beans should be sown broad cast over an acre, and the men afterwards to hoe amongst them as well as they can; this assertion, in opposition to the Kentish culture of that vegetable, is like quoting the ideas of the common Jamaica planters in answer to my argument. The moment the growth of a vegetable is known, every person, the least conversant in the different modes of husbandry, must be able to decide at once whether the horse-hoeing mode is well calculated for its culture; and when the sugar-cane is described, that is a strong reed, an inch diameter, and from four to eight feet high, will they not laugh at promiscuous planting and hand-hoeing which, comparatively speaking, is like hand-hoeing a grove of oaks. The article of culture known in England which most resembles sugar, is beans, and all our farmers who cultivate that crop to considerable profit agree, that the drill and horse-

horse-hoe is the only mode which can be attended with great success.

And here I shall make a few remarks on the conduct of the Jamaica planters in the management of their negroes, which may very justly be ranked among the errors of their husbandry.

In the account I gave of the culture of tobacco and rice by negroes, I had occasion to observe, that the stock of Blacks was there kept up by natural increase; and that the planters were all in the method of tasking their slaves; that is, they allotted them a portion of work every day, which the overseers attended to see well done, but never exacted a larger portion of labour. The management of Jamaica is very different: no task is there set, consequently the men know no end of their labour; they are followed throughout their work by the lower overseers with whips, exactly in the same manner as horses are in England, or if there is a diffe-ence, it is that the negroes are more hardly used. The consequence of this system is seen in the decrease of the stock; so that a plantation in Jamaica, which employs one hundred slaves, requires an annual supply of seven to keep up the number. This destruction
cannot

cannot be owing to climate, becaufe the coaft of Guinea is very fimilar, and the heat is never oppreffive to them; it is owing merely to exceffive work and bad ufage. Nothing can be clearer to common fenfe than the evidence of this fact.

The expences, profit and lofs of the fugar culture in this ifland have never been laid before the public with the leaft degree of accuracy; I have, by making repeated enquiries among Jamaica planters and agents, gained many particulars, which will enable me to give a very fatisfactory eftimate, and fuch as, I am clear, will yield more information than has by any other perfon been publifhed.

Calculation of a confiderable plantation in Jamaica.

	£.
600 acres of land purchafed at 11l. per acre,	6600
Two windmills, - - 1000	
Refervoir, &c. - - 260	
Boiling-houfe, coppers, &c. - 1350	
Curing-houfe, - - 460	
The ftove, &c. - - 180	
The ftill-houfe, &c. - - 180	
Sheds, - - - 90	
Stables, cattle-pens, &c. - 230	
Manfion and three other houfes, 1600	
	5350
Implements of all forts exclufive of fixtures,	500
10 negroes at an average of 120l. - -	1200
Carried over, £.	13,650

	Brought forward	£. 13,650
167 negroes at 50l.		8,350
100 head of cattle, 15l.		1,500
100 ditto at 10l.		1,000
30 mules at 25l.		750
100 swine, 15s.		75
		£. 25,325

One year's expence.

Overseer, managers, drivers, clerks, agent, farrier, &c.	650
9 negroes,	450
Expences on 177 ditto at 3l.	531
Repairs of buildings,	200
Wear and tear,	100
Cattle,	150
Lumber,	200
Taxes,	100
Sundries,	119
	2,500
	£. 27,825
Interest at 5 per cent.	1,391
	£. 29,216

If borrowed in Jamaica, the interest will be 8 per cent.

Product.

400 hogsheads of sugar of various sizes, but at an average of 15l.	6,000
Rum, 270 hhds.	2,434
	£. 8,434

Expence.

Sundries as above,	2,500
Profit,	5,934

which is 20l. 6s. per cent. on 29,216l.

This

This upon a very moderate average: the interest per cent. will vibrate from 15 to 30; and the planter, if he is very skilful, will carry this 20 to 25 at least; but he must in either case reside on the spot. And here it is necessary to remark, that less interest for a capital cannot be supposed in a climate highly insalubrious to European constitutions, and which is exposed to the most dreadful accidents of earthquakes and hurricanes: some allowance, indeed, is made for these in the preceding calculations, but such cannot be adequate, and excludes articles of entire destruction: that the interest is not less, we may also judge from the planters residing in England, leaving their estates to the management of agents, &c. and yet making from four to ten per cent. of their capital, according to their conduct and sagacity, which, all things considered, is a great proof that the culture must be very profitable. And I should further observe, that if more enlightened ideas were introduced into the modes of cultivating the cane, the profit would be far more considerable; I have no doubt but 40 per cent. on the capital might be made with as much or more ease than 25 at present. And the reader should note in this case of the sugar culture in Jamaica, as well

well as in all the branches of husbandry on the continent, that the part of the capital employed in the purchase of the estate pays as great interest as the rest of it, which is employed in the cultivation; an advantage no where to be met with in Europe. If a person engages in husbandry in England he may make a good profit on his farming, but as to the purchase of his estate he will not make above 2½ or 3 per cent. by it. Upon the whole I am inclined to believe, that the agriculture of sugar might be, of all other branches, the most profitable; and so it ought, for men who sacrifice themselves with such fortunes, in such a climate, ought surely to make a larger interest of their money than if they were employed in their native, or some wholesome climate *.

Besides sugar, this island produces some other staples which are or might be of very great importance. Among these cotton is a considerable article, the export amount-

---

* Since this was written a New History of Jamaica has appeared, which makes the interest 10 per cent. that is, 6 for interest paid, and 4 for the planter; but that this is very inadequate, every person, on reflection, must allow, for the planter must very soon be in gaol: if the circumstance of planters residing in England, and making 6 per cent. be considered, it will certainly be allowed, that on the spot it ought to be 20.

ing

ing to about 2000 bags; coffee, but nothing like what the French make in their islands; pimento; mahogany; cocoa was once a very great article, but it has much declined; indigo was once the staple of the island, but the attention now given to sugar has rendered all other articles of but small comparative account.

The following is an account of their exports.

	£.
48,515 hogsheads of sugar at 15l.	727,823
Rum and melasses,	433,591
Cotton 1626 bags at 10l. 15s.	17,479
Coffee 220 casks,	2,342
Pimento 438,000 lb.	15,632
Mahogany,	17,858
Sundries, as logwood nicarago, fustic, ligum vitæ, cocoa, ginger, canella, or winter's bark, peruvian bark, balsams, indigo, aloes, hides, staves, dry goods, bullion, &c.	32,140
Total, *	1,246,868

This is a prodigious sum for an island to produce, the cultivated part of which does not exceed three or four hundred thousand acres; but as the whole contains four millions, it ought to be a spur to our government to remedy the monstrous evil of such a proportion of it remaining waste; much is certainly incapable of culture, but the tracts of fine soil which would yield

---

* *Political Essays*, p. 286.

sugar, and the yet greater tracts which might be most profitably applied to the culture of other staples, are so many nuisances to the public, which deserve the most serious consideration: the monopolies of wastes are infinitely detrimental, and ought not only to be guarded against in future, but even remedied in past.

Settlements might be made most advantageously upon the lands in this island not yet granted away, if not for the culture of sugar, at least for those of other staples, such as cotton, indigo, cocoa, &c. which require small capitals, and would prove very profitable. A little management in government would bring such culture into more repute, and spread it through those waste tracts which are such a reproach to the nation.

There have of late years been a few very important improvements made in particular spots; but these, though reflecting great honour on individuals, are not of such extent as to remedy the evil of so large a portion of the island remaining uncultivated. Among these one deserves particular attention; it is the improvement Mr. K— wrought.

That gentleman purchased a swamp for a thousand pounds, which was at the time
of

of his purchase reckoned a very large price for it: his first work was to survey it carefully in order to mark out the drains that would be necessary to lay it dry. Having performed this with as much accuracy as possible, he cut a main drain, through the center of the swamp, into a navigable river, wide enough for canoes to pass and repass; by properly directing this drain, he found so much immediate service from it as to give him the greatest hope of success; this was a very heavy and expensive work to him, for at the time that he first planned the design of a drain, he had his eye on the convenience of a navigation in the future cultivation of the land.

When this main cut was finished, he began cross cuts, through the swamp on each side the main drain and communicating with it; these were of a something less dimension, but yet sufficient for navigating, and as fast as they were finished the swamp became nearly dry, and to appearance sound land: but this was rather deceitful, for upon the subsidence of the surface of the swamp he found it necessary to sink all his drains, which was a work of much trouble and expence.

Having completed a considerable part of the draining, he erected sugar works, with all

all the necessary buildings, upon the most convenient spot for that part of the swamp which was first dry, purchased negroes, and all things necessary, among which, however, cattle made but a small article. In this respect he made a wonderful use of his navigable cross cuts; by multiplying them from cross to cross he made them fully answer all the purposes of roads, and intervals between the divisions of the cane grounds: thus every article of *carriage* in the plantation was by this means transferred from negroes and mules to boats, even to that of the bundles of canes to the mills, &c. This contrivance rendered very few cattle necessary: respecting the object of raising manure, for which so many planters are obliged to sacrifice many other interests, this gentleman, from examining the soil of the swamp accurately, found it of so fertile and promising an appearance, that none would be necessary for many years, as the land looked as if the canes would rather be too luxuriant in their growth than not enough so; but as he also knew that such a quality is continually on the decrease after the land becomes cultivated, he made an ample provision for cattle, by bringing into tillage with the plough some of the larger divisions, and sowing them

them with Scotch grafs (panic), and other plants, so that the profitable part of cattle-keeping might at any time be practised, without the expence of supporting them merely for their work and dung; there is no part of the world in which cattle for provisions answer better than in Jamaica: this system therefore was answering every beneficial purpose that could be wished. It was executed by degrees as the other works went on.

When drained, the soil of the swamp was found to be a light hazel mould inclining to a peat, about eighteen inches deep, on a bed of stiff loam five feet deep, and under that a white clay: nothing could shew greater signs of inexhaustible fertility than the experiments made with several plants on the first division that was completely drained.

The first establishment for the purpose of planting was that of 100 negroes, with all the buildings requisite, and which was began before the first work of draining was in all parts finished. Nothing could exceed the crop which was reaped, and contrary to expectation the sugars proved of a very fine grain. Every working hand made three hogsheads, which was a produce that is but rarely met with. Every year, for six succeſſive ones, Mr. K—— increaſed his ſtock of negroes conſiderably, and the produce did not fail him in any one of them; ſo that the immenſe receipts from his plantation repaid him part of the expence of his drainage: when it was finiſhed, three hundred negroes more were thrown to planting, and the ſugars they made were ſuppoſed to exceed in quantity per head thoſe of any other plantation in the iſland.

Upon this great ſucceſs attending the undertaking, many perſons were deſirous of purchaſing parts of the ſwamp in order to convert them in like manner into ſugar plantations; but Mr. K—— was deſirous of having only one trouble with the whole, and offered it to ſale to any perſon or perſons that would bargain for the whole purchaſe. The event of the affair is perhaps the moſt extraordinary inſtance of improvement that was ever known: the whole, that is land, buildings, negroes, &c. were ſold for ONE HUNDRED THOUSAND POUNDS.

This vaſt ſum was to be paid by inſtallments, bearing intereſt 8 per cent. till paid. In the valuation the land was reckoned at 60l. an acre, and the negroes at 60l. each, one with another. The following account

is

is not absolutely accurate, but the particulars are not far from the truth.

	£.
Produce of the sale,	100,000
Profit on the planting, after the improvement, during seven years,	32,000
Total receipt, £.	132,000
Purchase, £. 1000	
Drainage, expence in negroes, &c. 27500	
Buildings, 13000	
Negroes, 14700	
Implements, 2080	
Cattle and sundries, 7500	
	65,780
Clear profit,	66,220

It is very much to the honour of this sensible gentleman that he had sagacity enough to understand the advantages which might be made by draining such a swamp: his plan, before the execution, was treated as a visionary scheme by all the old planters, who laughed at the project, and foretold the ruin of the undertaker. The work turning out so successfully will have most beneficial consequences: there are other swamps in the island equally accessible, of the same soil, and as easily to be drained; all which circumstances are clear from the almost immediate rise in the price of such lands upon the success of Mr. K——; and some other undertakings of the same kind

kind have been begun, from which there is reason to expect a similar success.

Improvements of this and other kinds are more wanting in Jamaica than in any of our other islands, for here we have the largest territory we possess in the West Indies. Not above a fourth of this island being patented, and not a fourth of that fourth under any sort of culture, ought to instigate men to more activity, and a more acute examination of the districts in this island, which have been hitherto rejected or neglected. Doubtless there are many extensive tracts among them, which might be applied to sugar, if planters would, like the gentleman who executed the above improvement, apply to raising that commodity in new methods, varied and adapted to circumstances in the soil and situation not usual in the old plantations.

CHAP.

CHAP. XXX.

BARBADOES.

Climate — Soil — Productions — Exports — Observations on the culture of sugar in Barbadoes.

THIS little island, deservedly one of the most famous in the world, is situated in 13 degrees north latitude: it is about twenty-five miles in length, and in breadth fourteen, containing one hundred and forty square miles, and by supposition 100,000 acres. The climate is in some respects preferable to that of Jamaica, and in others inferior: the face of the country on the coast is higher and more free from low grounds and swamps, much of it being quite walled with rocks; this makes the air drier, and consequently healthier; but the nights are hotter from the want of the land breeze, which in Jamaica is owing to the mountains, and Barbadoes having none cannot possess this advantage; but upon the whole, the climate is reckoned superior to that of the other island.

The soil is generally a light hazel loam, of a dark or reddish colour, with exceptions for stiffer tracts; it is in every spot of the island capable of bearing some valuable product or other; contrary to Jamaica, every inch being under cultivation. Of their products, sugar is the grand article; indigo they still cultivate; ginger is a very good article; they have some cotton and pimento. Among their other products they reckon oranges, lemons, citrons, pomegranates, pine apples, guavas, plantains, cocoa nuts, Indian figs, prickly pears, melons, &c. In general, the produce of the island is as rich as any other in the West Indies.

The great value of it to this country will appear clearly from the progress of its trade and export. In 1650, which was only twenty years after its first settlement, it contained between 30 and 40,000 white inhabitants, and a yet larger number of blacks. Upon the Restoration the colony granted 4½ per cent. duty on its exports towards maintaining the forts and fortifications, but which has been shamefully misapplied to other purposes.

It

It is very remarkable, that the people of this island spent forty years in raising indigo, ginger, cotton, and tobacco; and then learnt of the Portugueze at Brazil the art of planting the sugar cane, and this acquisition in no longer space than ten years totally changed the face of affairs in the island: the planters who were before in but low circumstances, became remarkably wealthy.

In 1676 the island was at its meridian; by a calculation that was made with great exactness there were then found in it 50,000 white people of all sorts, and 80,000 negroes: this was a degree of population truly amazing. The author of the *European Settlements in America* justly observes, that Holland itself, or perhaps even the best inhabited parts of China, were never peopled to the same proportion; and Dr. Campbell remarks, with equal truth, that never any colony of ours, or any other nation, was so populous as this: and to make this still clearer to an English reader, we shall observe, that Barbadoes is rather less than the county of Rutland, the smallest county in England, and that according to the highest computation, the number of people in that county in 1676 did not exceed 20,000.

But

But this may be made still clearer by comparing that whole island with this in point of extent; for if England and Wales taken together consist of near forty millions of acres, then if they were as populous as Barbadoes, they ought to contain fifty millions of people—whereas Sir William Petty, who was a very able man in computation, and is thought not to have undervalued this country, but rather the contrary, never reckoned the people higher than eight millions, which shews what a vast disproportion there is between the peopling of the two countries. But to proceed farther still; the same great man asserts, that in Holland and Zealand, which are looked upon to be the best peopled countries in Europe, there are a million of souls inhabiting about as many acres; and consequently it appears from hence, that even this country was not so well peopled as Barbadoes.

At present the number of whites are computed to be near 30,000, but the slaves amount to about 100,000. About the same time that the population was at its height, so also was its wealth. In the year 1661 King Charles II. created on the same day thirteen baronets in Barbadoes, none of them

them having less than one thousand pounds, and some of them ten thousand pounds a year. At this time their trade actually maintained four hundred sail of ships, one with another of 150 tons; their annual exported produce in sugar, indigo, ginger, cotton, &c. amounted to upwards of 350,000l. and their circulation cash at home was 200,000l. These are facts that may be depended upon, that deserve in every respect the greatest consideration, and that plainly demonstrate at once the great value of this island, and the prodigious consequence of our plantations in general [*].

Let us exclude all that accrued from Barbadoes to the people of England before the Restoration, and estimate its produce from 1660 to 1760 at 16,000 hogsheads of sugar, which make 12,000 ton annually, and omitting entirely the rum or spirits, melasses, cotton, ginger, aloes, and all the other commodities of the island, estimating this at 20l. a ton, it will amount to 240,000 l. per ann. or 24,000,000 l. in the course of the century either gained or saved to this nation, which, considering

---

[*] *Harris's Voyages*, vol. ii. p. 256.

that

that Barbadoes is not bigger than the *Isle of Wight*, must appear a most amazing sum; and yet in proof of the modesty of this computation it would be easy to name a very intelligent author, who before the close of the last century affirmed, that no less than thirty millions had been gained by our possession of Barbadoes at the time he wrote. But though his zeal might possibly carry him a little too far then, there is not now the least room to question that the very best judges, by which is to be understood those who are best versed in these kind of things, and who also best understand this trade, would more readily concur in fixing the amount of our profits during the period before assigned, at thirty than at twenty-four millions *.

As to the present produce of this island, the following is the best account we have had.

	£.
Sugar, 20,266 hogsheads, at 15l.	303,990
Rum and melasses,	203,992
Sundry articles, such as ginger, cotton, indigo, sweetmeats, aloes, cassia,	30,000
	£. 537,982

---

* *Considerations on the Sugar Trade*, p. 27.

But

But in this account is included all the rum that can be made from the total of melasses: I think that article too high: if 100,000l. is allowed for rum, the total will amount to above 400,000l. a year. The custom-house books for 1763 make the British imports from this island above 300,000 l. if to this North America is added, the total, probably, would be as large as above mentioned.

Considering that the export of only 400,000l. a year amounts to 4l. annually for every acre in the whole island, and as towns, roads, water, rocks, &c. which yield no produce must necessarily reduce the 100,000 acres considerably, it would amount probably to 4l. 10s. upon the cultivated part of the soil: and considering further that a large portion of the food of the people, both whites and blacks, is raised upon the island, and also that the planters are obliged to keep many cattle, the principal part of whose subsistence grows there, it will be evident that a large part of it is applied to other uses besides yielding the exported produce: further considering that a third part of all the cane grounds is fallow every year, and it will then appear that the part of the island actually

ally yielding exportable produce is small in comparison of the whole, I should not imagine that more than 25,000 acres in that situation, consequently the produce per acre is 15l. But whatever produce is taken, most certainly agriculture never flourished in any country in the world equally with what it has done here: for many years it has been on the decline, not in the value of its produce, for that is as great as ever, but in the *quantity* of it: in the last century they made, it has been asserted, more sugar than at present, consequently the real product of the island was once greater even than the above account: it is the rise in the prices of their commodities that has kept up the total value of their products. But let me slightly remark, that I recollect no particular accounts of the exports in the last century, which shews any decline at present even in the quantity.

Relative to the culture of the sugar-cane in this island, there is no material difference between their method and that described under the last article. But the Barbadoes planter labours under greater difficulties and larger expences. The soil of the island has been so long employed in yielding crops,

crops, that it requires more dung than the fresh grounds in Jamaica; it is not worn out, as many superficial writers have asserted, for a good soil never wears out; bad management in the culture of sugar, as well as in any other branch of culture, will exhaust the soil, and it will be inferior till good management restores it. But as long as the planters conduct themselves upon rational principles they will find the produce of their island great as ever. As to the fertility of fresh lands, it is exhausted much sooner than commonly imagined: planters are too apt to take liberties with such land, and pour in a succession of crops in haste to reap the benefit of the goodness of the land, without giving it sufficient rest, or changing their system: when this is the case, the fertility of new lands is gone in ten or dozen years, and they will be even inferior to neighbouring tracts that have been in culture a century, but managed upon good principles.

In these there is nothing of greater importance than manuring; this they understand very well in Barbadoes, where every planter keeps considerable stocks of cattle merely with a view to the dung they raise him. They confine them to pens, in which they

they are fed, that all their dung, urine, and waste of food may be retained in a bed of marle, which they spread in each pen; at certain seasons they mix the heap well together, and find it a mass of manure admirably calculated for the improvement of their land; superior even to what a similar quantity of dung alone would be. This I attribute to the marle retaining the juices of the dung, and parting with them gradually to the roots of the successive crops. Nor has the sun (which in this hot climate is a material point) near such power to exhale the beneficial parts of the manure when united with an absorbent earth, as it has upon dung alone.

The great difficulty of the planters is in supporting cattle sufficient for the purpose of raising the requisite body of manure: the smallness of the island, which is so crammed with people, denies them the extensive savannahs or meadows which they possess in Jamaica; their crops of Scotch grass are not near so great, nor have they the land to spare for it of the right sort; their dependance therefore is principally on cane-tops and the leaves of Indian corn, both which they feed with green, and also make into large ricks in hay. But if they would

would be persuaded to cultivate lucerne, they would surely reap great benefit from it in the support of their cattle, than which they have no object more essential. The length of the root would secure the plant from the sun, probably when its beams were most violent, and afford, through the heats of summer, fresh crops of green food every month regularly for the cattle: this is what they most want, for at that season all their grass is burnt up, and, contrary to the practice of colder climates, the summer is the season for feeding with dry fodder, and the winter that for green. Lucerne therefore would prove of the highest advantage to them.

Another article in their management, which might be much improved, is the arrangement of their grounds for crops: the cane grounds they keep under canes for ever, with only the assistance of fallow and dung. But on the contrary, the canes should be planted by turns on all the lands of a plantation: sometimes a field should be under grass; sometimes yams, plantains, garden plants, cotton, indigo, &c. &c. at others fallow; and at others under canes, &c. This change of crop would be of great service, the canes would in the succession have the advantage of what may, to them, be called fresh land; and less dung would do than when they are planted always in the same spot.

Nothing hardly is more profitable to a planter than yams, potatoes, and plantains; and these three crops have the same effect in meliorating the soil and preparing it by their shade, for exhausting crops, as potatoes, clover, pease, &c. have in England: nothing therefore can be better management than to make a change of product the foundation for sugar. Let grass lands, when of a proper age, be broken up for those roots, &c. and let the roots be succeeded by canes; after canes, other staples, corn, &c. then fallow, and upon that canes again, then grasses, &c. By means of such a system the food for cattle would be much increased, all the lands of an estate kept in good order, the grasses superior to the common ones, and the canes from such a change would yield more plentifully.

CHAP.

CHAP. XXXI.

LEEWARD ISLANDS.

Antigua—St. Chriftopher's—Nevis—Montferrat — Barbuda —Anguilla — Climate —Soil—Products — Exports —Agriculture—Obfervations.

ANTIGUA, or Antego, as it is fometimes written, lies in 16 degrees 11 minutes north latitude. It is circular in its form, being about twenty miles in diameter and fixty in circumference, containing about 70,000 acres of land. The climate is inferior to that of Barbadoes, being hotter, and is reckoned more fubject to hurricanes. Only a part of it is yet cleared, being in many places covered with its original woods; a circumftance to the benefit of the prefent planters in many refpects. The face of the country in one refpect is very fingular; there is neither a brook, rivulet, or fpring in the whole ifland, which obliges the inhabitants to depend on artificial ponds, cifterns, and refervoirs of water for all their ufes. Threatening as this was originally, experience has removed the difficulties which flowed from it, and they have been able to supply themselves very regularly with this necessary of life.

The soil of the island is generally sandy, but not therefore infertile; on the contrary, there are nowhere more flourishing sugar plantations to be met with than in this island; for there is a loamy mixture in the sand which keeps it from burning; and the reddish earths, though sandy, are found excellent cane lands. The produce of the island has been thus stated:

	£.
15,500 hhds. sugar at 15l.	232,500
Rum, - - -	63,933
Sundry articles, - -	10,000
£.	306,433

These sundry articles are ginger, a little indigo and tobacco, fruits and other things, common in all the islands; but the quantities are but small, and I should rather think 10,000 l. too great an allowance for them. We have no island in the West Indies, Jamaica and the ceded ones excepted, that is capable of such improvement as Antigua: indeed the industry of its owners

owners has carried their agriculture to a much greater height than it was ever expected they would attain; for the time was when Antigua sugars could find no market in Britain, but were sold at low prices to Hamburgh and the North. A very great change has been made since, for at present we do not often see finer muscovado sugar than comes from this island. The improvements to be made are principally those of bringing into culture the lands yet waste or underwood; most of which, it is not doubted, but will produce good sugar, perhaps from freshness superior to the old plantations; if this measure was well effected, we should annually receive from Antigua 20,000 hogsheads of sugar, and a much greater quantity of rum would be made than is at present, proportionably to the quantity of sugar.

St. Christopher's is situated in 17 deg. 25 min. north latitude; it is about seventy-five miles in circuit, yet are there not in it above 24,000 acres of land that can ever be brought to yield sugar, for part of it is covered with very high mountains. The soil is remarkable for producing the finest sugars in the West Indies; it is a light, hazel

zel mould on brick earth, of a surprising fertility, which soil is justly supposed to be of all others the best for producing sugar. The climate is as agreeable and temperate as any other island in that hot latitude. The products are,

	£.
10,000 hhds. of sugar at 15l. a hhd.	150,000
Rum, - - -	41,250
Sundries, - -	7,000
Total, £.	198,250

I have had an account of a small plantation in this island given me, which it is proper to introduce here. It is as follows. One hundred and ten acres of land, only part of which is fit for sugar, with a small mansion, one mill, and a proportioned sett of buildings, coppers, &c. were purchased about five years ago for the sum of

	£.
	3200
Paid for the implements, &c. at the same time,	113
For 47 seasoned negroes at 62l. a head, -	2914
For cattle, &c. - - -	640
£.	6867

The gentleman who made the purchase left i to the management of an agent, who also had the care of some other plantations. He

He has generally shipped him 60 hogsheads of sugar a year, and 26 hogsheads of rum.

	l. s. d.
60 hdds. sugar at 15l.	900 0 0
26 rum at 9l.	234 0 0
Total receipt,	1134 0 0

Deduct.

Interest of 6867l. at 5 per cent.	343 0 0	
Agent's bill of charges,	655 10 0	
		998 10 0
Neat proceeds,		135 10 0

Hence it appears that the planter in Enggland gains only 2 per cent. for his money more than he may be supposed to pay for it, or 7 per cent. which for a security any ways hazardous, and that of every plantation is much so, must be reckoned miserable interest for his money. This, however, is not owing to the fault of sugar, but of agency: plantations that are left to the conduct of agents and overseers, generally turn out so. There is reason to believe from this instance, as well as many others, that greater extortioners are hardly to be met with than West India agents, attornies, and overseers, who generally take such advantage of the distant residence of their employers as to make those estates carry the worst

worst aspect, which ought in fact to be highly valued. But it is farther curious to see the profit they allow their masters, which is just calculated to prevent their selling their estates, when themselves shall borrow money in the islands at 8 and even 9 per cent. to throw into a business, from which they remit the owners no more than 7! The truth is, planting sugar upon the fine soil of St. Christopher's will, with proper management, pay from 25 to 35 per cent. for the money employed; but then residence is necessary; for as to living in London by agriculture in the West Indies, it is an impracticable scheme to unite such contraries with profit.

St. Christopher's was many years ago in a very thriving condition; as may be gathered from the sale of the French lands in the island, after the cession of their part of it at the peace of Utrecht, produced so large a sum, that the princess of Orange's marriage portion of eighty thousand pounds was paid out of it.

NEVIS is situated so near St. Christopher's as to be separated from it only by a narrow channel; it is about six miles across, and near twenty in circumference;
for

for want of the high lands of St. Kitt's, the climate is not so good, nor is the soil reckoned quite equal to it; yet is this small island inhabited by 5000 whites and 12,000 blacks; a great number for so little a spot, and shews how completely cultivated most of it must be. Its produce is,

	£.
6000 hogsheads of sugar at 15l.	90,000
2000 hogsheads rum at 9l.	18,000
Sundries,	3,000
Total, £.	111,000

The island of MONTSERRAT lies in 17° north lat.; it is about nine miles long, and nearly of the same breadth. There is no part of the West Indies that is more healthy or agreeable than this little island. There are some high mountains in it which cool and refresh the air by a land-breeze; and these being at the same time well covered with tall cedar and other wood, the shade afforded is delicious, as well as the prospect it yields lovely. The vallies are extremely fertile, yielding all the West Indian productions in perfection; and they are at the same time well watered. The number of white inhabitants in the island is about 4500,

4500, and the slaves 12,000. The product is about 3500 hogsheads of sugar; but it is on the improving hand both in population and product.

	£.
3500 hogsheads at 15l.	52,500
1110 hogsheads rum at 9l.	9,900
Sundries,	1,500
Total, £.	63,900

BARBUDA lies in 17 deg. 30 min. north latitude; it is about fifteen miles long. The climate is not equal to that of Montserrat, from the lowness of the lands. The soil is very fertile, yet the inhabitants have not gone upon sugar; this has not been from any defect in the soil, climate, or situation, but has been owing to that degree of custom and habit which are so apt to govern mankind. Long after our first settling this island the native Caribbees remained in it, and more than once burnt and plundered the new settlements; this deterred every body from erecting and establishing such expensive and hazardous works as those for sugar; but after the natives were carried off the island, this motive ceased, and the conduct should have ceased like-

likewife; but the people being got into the courfe of common hufbandry, they knew not how to quit it: the beft part of the ifland was in hands who, from their eafe and comfort of their life, would not part with their farms, which excluded new comers from introducing fugar; and thus has the ifland continued to the prefent time applied almoft entirely to raifing corn and provifions, principally the breeding of cattle. The neighbourhood of the fugar iflands, with whom alone they have any connection, affords them a certain and good market for every thing they have to fell. The number of people in the ifland is about 1500, among whom are very few negroes. The property of the ifland is in the Codrington family, the head of which puts in a governor at Barbuda, having the fame prerogatives the other lords proprietors in their feveral jurifdictions in America. Their anceftor, colonel Chriftopher Codrington, governor of Barbadoes, who dying in 1710, gave two plantations in Barbadoes, and part of this ifland, valued in the whole at 2000l. per ann. to the fociety for the propagation of the Gofpel, for the inftruction of the negroes in Barbadoes, and the reft of the Carribbee iflands islands in the Christian religion, and for erecting and endowing a college in Barbadoes. This great man was a native of Barbadoes, and, as has been well observed, for a great number of amiable and useful qualities both in public and private life, for his courage and his zeal for the good of his country, his humanity, his knowledge, and love of literature, was far the richest production and most shining ornament Barbadoes ever had.

I before observed, that the people of Barbuda addicted themselves to breeding and feeding cattle, and raising corn. Their meadows are some of them very fine ones, abounding plentifully with those grasses which in the West Indies are found most profitable: their herds are not large, from the division of property, but very numerous: having many cows and young cattle, horses and asses, for breeding mules, some sheep, and particularly swine; the products of America are peculiarly adapted for rearing and feeding hogs; most of the trees yield plenty of mast; the leaves of many of their succulent vegetables do well for them, and the products of roots much exceed any thing in Europe. An acre of potatoes and yams in Barbuda will yield as much

much as three or four acres of potatoes in England. Their method of planting them in this ifland is thus: they plough the land three times, and then carrying on such manure as they have, mark the field by line into ftripes of five feet broad; on each fide the line, at the diftance of eight inches from it, they lay a row of potatoe fetts, and as they proceed cover them with earth, taken with fhovels from the fpaces between the lines. Planters lefs attentive will do the fame work without lines, but then their land is far from having any neat appearance. As the crop grows they keep earthing it up in the fame manner, quite through the fummer; and when they take up their roots, they do it with fpades or forks: as to the produce, I have been affured they fometimes get from one acre of land up to fifty-three or fifty-four tons, and that from thirty-five to forty are common crops. It is eafy to conceive what a fource of profit fuch products muft be, where potatoes bear a conftant price, as they do all over the Weft Indies; and to what advantage the people of this ifland may breed fwine upon the very offal of fuch crops.

The

The way of life among the farmers of Barbuda resembles that of the little freeholders in New England; these also having the property of their farms, seldom renting them from others. Each man has his comfortable dwelling, and his well inclosed fields around it, a fine grove of trees for shelter, his orchard and garden filled with delicious fruits, his meadows for his herds, some lands for Indian, called here Guinea Corn, and others for roots, &c. Considering the vast plenty which husbandry in such a climate yields of almost every thing, it may truly be said these little farmers lead a life very much superior to that of their little brethren in Europe.

Anguilla is situated in 18 deg. 12 min. north latitude; it is thirty miles long by ten broad, and is in every respect too fine an island to be left in the condition we see it. There are not above 800 people in it, who are to be divided into two classes; one a set of industrious farmers (like those of Barbuda), among whom there was a few years ago one or two sugar works, and the other a set of lazy people who live like Indians, pursuing no other occupation than that of tending a few herds, and living on them

them and the spontaneous fruits of the island. It is very remarkable, and indeed is a circumstance of curiosity, that there is no government in this island, every head of a family being truly a sovereign, and yet the settled part of the inhabitants live in peace and security, notwithstanding the wandering class, who know neither law nor gospel. This seems a great contradiction; but so it is.

The farmers in this island principally follow the planting Indian corn, in which they have good success, and sell considerable quantities of it to the sugar islands: their crops are reckoned very good: they also plant some tobacco, which, after neglecting for many years, they have lately taken up again, but the quantity is not considerable. Great improvements might be made, if a deputy governor was fixed here with a regular civil government; which it has been apprehended would draw people of property to make purchases in the island, with a view to plant sugar; for there are large tracts of land in it of a fine sandy loam, of a reddish colour, which resembles the brick earth of Jamaica, and which in its fertility in

the

the production of such crops as the people plant, shews how excellently it would do for sugar. The scarcity and dearness of land in our islands make it the more surprising that this has never been done.

CHAP.

CHAP. XXXII.

CEDED ISLANDS.

Dominica—St. Vincent—Granada—Tobago —Importance of these islands—Their produce—Improvements—Observations.

BY the peace of Paris we procured the cession, or rather the confirmation, of our right to these islands; the degree of merit that treaty possesses on this account does not turn on the value of these acquisitions, but on our degree of right to them before; and as that enquiry is not connected with the subject of this work, I shall dismiss the idea of it; but proceed to describe them, as well as the imperfect accounts we have had will allow, with the assistance of such private information as I have been able to gain, some of which has been valuable.

DOMINICA lies in 15° 30′ north lat. between Martinico and Guadalupe; it is twenty-eight miles long by thirteen broad, and in circumference about ninety: it is supposed to be about twice as large as Barbadoes. The air, except in some places that are marshy and overgrown with wood, is generally reputed wholesome. There is no doubt but when the island is cleared it will, like the rest, become still more healthy, or at least more agreeable to European constitutions. The face of the country is rough and mountainous, more especially towards the sea side, but within land, there are many rich and fine vallies, and some large and fair plains. The declivities of the hills are commonly gentle, so as to facilitate their cultivation, and the soil almost every where a deep black mould, and thence highly commended for its fertility by the Spanish, English, and French. It is excellently well watered by at least thirty rivers, some, and particularly one of them is very large and navigable for several miles, and the rest very commodious for all the purposes of planting. Hogs, both wild and tame, are here in great abundance, as well as all sorts of fowls, and ground provisions, such as bananas, potatoes, manioc; none of the islands produce better. Their fruits also are excellent, and the settlements, which however were not numerous, which the French made upon the island, flourished very much, and produced sugar, cotton, coffee, cocoa, and most

most of the articles common in the West Indies *.

Since it has come into our possession, a considerable progress has been made in cultivating it: many tracts of lands have been purchased, and sugar-works erected on them. Insomuch that in 1763, only a year after the peace, the export from the island to Great Britain amounted to 46,211l. 17s. 9d. a very considerable sum for so short a time after the possession. Since that time the products have increased considerably, so that at present it is one of the most beneficial islands we have; insomuch that last year its exports amounted to above two hundred thousand pounds.

St. Vincent lies in the same atitude as Barbadoes, at the distance of only thirty leagues. It is from north to south twenty miles long, and in breadth about twelve; the circumference being about sixty miles. It is something larger than Antigua. The warmth of the climate is so tempered with the sea-breezes, that it is looked upon as very healthy and agreeable, and on the eminences, which are numerous, the air is rather cool. The soil is wonderfully fertile,

---

* *Considerations on the Nature of the Sugar Trade.*

though

though the country is hilly, and in some places mountainous. But amongst the former, there are some pleasant vallies, and at the bottom of the latter, some spacious and luxuriant plains. No island of the same extent is better watered with rivers and streams, yet are there no marshes nor stagnant waters. There are here great quantities of fine timber, and excellent fruit trees, some peculiar to this island. It abounds with wild sugar-canes, corn, rice, and all sorts of ground provisions. In the south part of the island, where the French have raised some spacious and flourishing settlements, they have coffee, indigo, cocoa, anatto, and some very fine tobacco. They have likewise abundance of cattle and poultry, and send from thence *lignum vitæ* and other kinds of timber to Martinico, where they were employed in building houses and in their fortifications. We may collect, that if this country was thoroughly and regularly cultivated, it would, in respect of its produce, be very little, if at all inferior to any of the islands that we already possess.

But there is one circumstance very capitally in disfavour of this otherwise excellent island, which must not be overlooked;
it

it is the number of native Indians and free negroes that are in possession of it. In the year 1735 it appeared, by an authentic report that was then made to the government of Barbadoes, that according to the best information, which could be at that juncture obtained, there were about six hundred French, four thousand Indians, and six thousand negroes in St. Vincent's: it is, however, said, that the numbers have since been much decreased, owing to a cruel war breaking out between the Indians and negroes, which lasted for many years [*].

Several reasons have been brought to shew, that so far from esteeming these prior inhabitants a disadvantage, we ought to reckon them a valuable acquisition. But such arguments are far enough from being founded in fact or experience. The author of the *Considerations* says as much on this head as can be said; but in spite of all that can be advanced, practical men know well enough, that till an island is clear of Indians and free negroes, no sugar can be planted to advantage. The instance of the Jamaica negroes proves this, rather than contradicts it, as may be seen by any person, who reflects on the immense losses,

---

[*] *Considerations, &c.*

expences, and trouble it coſt that iſland not to extirpate, but make a peace with a handful of men; and the example of the French proves the ſame thing, for though no iſland can be more favourable in ſoil and climate to ſugar, than St. Vincent's, yet did they not, though at peace with both Indians and negroes, venture upon that culture; confining themſelves to proviſions and other articles that required little expence. But if this reaſoning ſhould not be ſatisfactory, what are we to think of the tranſactions now going on in this iſland, which in the violation of the natural rights of mankind are of ſuch a hue, as to have brought on the enquiry now before parliament*? It ſhews plainly enough, that the iſland was of no worth while poſſeſſed even in part by the natives, and that in order to render it valuable, means had been taken which it is to be feared will make but a bad appearance in the face of day.

The iſland of GRANADA lies in 11 deg. 30 min. north latitude, the fartheſt to the ſouth of any of the Antilles. It is upwards of thirty miles long, and about half as many broad, being ſeventy-five in circumference. It is twice as large as Barbadoes, and con-

---

* This was written at the time of the enquiry into the affair of St. Vincent's.

tains

tains one third as much land fit for culture as is to be found in Martinico. The climate, as may be supposed from the latitude, is very hot, yet is it refreshed by the sea-breeze; it is well known to be as wholesome as any other island in these parts; notwithstanding the fever which has gone under the name of this island, but which is owing to the thickness of the woods, and of course declines every day. The seasons, as they are styled in the West Indies, are remarkably regular; the blast is not hitherto known; the inhabitants are not liable to many diseases that are epidemic in Martinico and Guadaloupe; and, which is the happiest circumstance of all, it lies out of the tract of the hurricanes, which, with respect to the safety of the settlements on shore, and the security of navigation, is almost an inestimable benefit.

There are in Grenada some very high mountains, but the number is small, and the eminences scattered through it are in general rather hills, gentle in their ascent, of no great height, fertile, and very capable of cultivation. But exclusive of these, there are on both sides the island large tracts of level ground, very fit for improvement, the soil being almost every where deep, rich, mellow, and fertile in the highest degree, so as to be equal in all respects, if not superior, to that of any of the islands in the West Indies, if the concurrent testimonies both of French and British planters may be relied upon. The former indeed have constantly, in their applications to the French ministry, insisted, that this might be very easily made one of the most valuable, though hitherto it has remained the weakest and the worst settled of all their colonies. It is perfectly well watered by many streams of different sizes; there are also smaller brooks running from most of the hills. The great produce of the country before our cultivation in it, and indeed partly since, is a prodigious variety of all the different sorts of timber that are to be met with in any of the West India islands, and all these excellent in their respective kinds; so that whenever it comes to be tolerably cleared, vast profits will arise from the timber that may be cut down, and for which markets will not be wanting. Cattle, fowls, and provisions, are in the utmost plenty. But the distinguishing excellency of Grenada does not lie simply in its great fertility, or in its fitness for a vast variety of valuable commodities, but in the peculiar quality of its soil, which gives a surprising and incontestible perfection to all its several productions. The sugar of Grenada is of a fine grain, and of course more valuable than that either of Martinico or Guadaloupe. The indigo is the finest in all the West Indies. While tobacco remained the staple commodity, as once it was of these islands, one pound of Granada tobacco was worth two or three that grew in any of the rest. The cocoa and cotton have an equal degree of pre-eminence. For some years before it came into our hands, the French planters in this island sent home twelve thousand hogsheads of sugar annually, besides coffee, cocoa, and a large quantity of excellent cotton. Yet it is generally allowed, that never one half of the country was properly settled that might have been obtained, if the inhabitants had been better planters, and had been also better supplied with slaves. An English gentleman, who has had great opportunities of knowing, thinks as much sugar is raised here as in Barbadoes, which is not at all impossible, though it did not find a regular passage to France. The Grenadines run from the southern extremity of the isle of Grenada;

nada; they are twenty-three small islands, capable of cultivation, the soil being remarkably rich, the climate pleasant, and all the necessaries of life, as fast as they are settled, easily obtained. According to the sentiments of the best judges, large quantities of indigo, coffee, and cotton may be raised upon them, nor are they at all unfit for sugar. Besides these, there are five larger islands, generally comprehended under the title of the Grenadines, *Cariouacou, Union, Cannouan, Moskito* island, and *Bequia*, called by the French Little Martinico. The first is of a circular figure, six or seven leagues in compass; it has been represented, by those who have visited it, as one of the finest and most fruitful spots in America; the soil remarkably fertile, and from its being pervaded by the sea-breeze, the climate equally wholesome and pleasant. It is covered with valuable timber, interspersed with rich fruit trees, and when settled and cultivated is capable of all kinds of improvement; and it has also the advantage of as deep, capacious, and commodious an harbour as any in the West Indies. *Union* is three leagues long. *Cannouan* is three leagues long, and one and an half broad. *Moskito* is three long and one broad.

broad. All of them very pleasant and fertile islands. *Bequia* is the largest, being thirty-six miles in circumference, consequently larger than Montserrat: the soil is equal, if not superior to any of the rest, but it has little fresh water, and abounds with venomous reptiles *.

As a strong proof that these representations were well founded, I shall remark, that Grenada and its dependencies sent home in 1763, to the British market, only sugar and other commodities, to the amount of 206,889 l. which tallies extremely well with the above mentioned product of 12,000 hogsheads of sugar. St. Kitt's produces 10,000, and its total export 198,250 l. consequently 12,000 must at least be equal to 206,889 l. Since that time our people have made a wonderful progress in planting this island: many very capital plantations have been established by gentlemen in England of the largest property, and the success which has attended, and is daily attending, such as reside on their estates in this island, and at the same time understand the business of planting, shews clearly that in a few years this will

---

* *Considerations, &c.*

be one of the moſt valuable ſettlements we have in the Weſt Indies. I have been favoured with an account of one plantation, which I ſhall lay before the reader, as in ſeveral points it is very ſatisfactory.

	£.
Purchaſe of 350 acres of land for canes (200 cleared) and 95 of woodland in the hills for raiſing proviſions, &c.	2,560
Manſion and one ſet of buildings,	2,600
Utenſils,	480
200 negroes at 56l. on an average,	11,200
Cattle,	320
£.	17,160

One year's expence.

Expences on 200 negroes, including overſeers, 4l. a head.	800
Repairs of buildings,	90
Wear and tear,	100
Cattle,	40
Taxes,	32
Extra charges,	86
Supply of negroes,	460
	1,608
£.	18,768

Product.

89 hogſheads ſugar, at 19l.	1,691
70 at 18l.	1,260
276 at 15l.	4,140
	7,091
200 hhds. of rum,	1,800
Carried over, £.	8,891

	Brought forward,	£.	8,891
Timber and fundry articles,			75
Total,		£.	8,966
Annual expence,			1,608
Annual profit,			7,358

This is near 39 per cent. interest of the capital, but it was drawn up from the particulars of an extraordinary year: while the poffeffor was on the plantation himfelf, he made near 27 per cent. since he has been in England, his neat produce is only 9 per cent. a frefh inftance of the lofs attending any perfon poffeffing eftates in the WeftIndia iflands without living upon them.

There is a very great error in the culture of the new lands in this ifland, which is the clearing them of wood in fuch a manner as to exclude the ufe of the plough: this has been the cafe with all our iflands, but the new fettlers in Granada have, through an eagernefs for profit, left the ftumps fo thick that no plough can be ufed; and even for hoes, by the accounts I have received, the inconvenience muft be great. It is much to be regretted that they will not beftow a little extra expence upon this article in their firft undertaking, and at the fame time determine upon intro-

ducing

ducing horse-culture in every branch of their agriculture where it is practicable. Another circumstance of consequence, and which demands equal attention, is their making free with the fertility of the fresh lands so much as our planters are too apt to do; the consequence of which will be, exhausting them in a few years, and then they will be in a worse state than if the soil under good management had not been of a comparable richness.

TOBAGO lies a little to the south-east of Granada; it is thirty-two miles long, and about nine broad, being seventy miles in circumference; it is rather larger than Barbadoes. The climate, though it lies only eleven degrees and ten minutes north from the equator, is not near so hot as might be expected, the force of the sun's rays being tempered by the coolness of the sea-breeze. When it was first inhabited, it was thought unhealthy, but as soon as it was a little cleared and cultivated, it was found to be equally pleasant and wholesome, which the Dutch ascribed, in a great measure, to the odoriferous smell exhaled from the spice and rich gum trees, a notion borrowed from their countrymen in the East Indies,

who

who are perſuaded that cutting down the clove trees in the Moluccas has rendered thoſe iſlands very unhealthy. Another circumſtance which may recommend the climate, is the iſland's lying out of the track of the hurricanes. There are many riſing grounds over all the iſland, but it cannot be properly ſtyled mountainous. The ſoil is very finely diverſified, being in ſome places light and ſandy, in others mixed with gravel and ſmall flints, but in general it is a deep, rich, black mould. Hardly any country can be better watered than Tobago, for beſides ſprings that are found in plenty all over the iſland, there are not fewer than eighteen rivulets that run from the hills into the ſea; but there are very few or no moraſſes or marſhes, or any lakes, pools, or collections of ſtanding waters, which of courſe muſt render it more healthy. It is covered with all that vaſt variety of timber that is to be found in moſt countries in the Weſt Indies, and many of theſe as extraordinary in ſize as excellent in their nature. The ſame may be ſaid with reſpect to fruit trees, and amongſt theſe there are ſome that are peculiar to Tobago; ſuch, for inſtance, as the true nutmeg tree, which the Dutch, who of all nations could not in that respect be deceived, affirm to have found here. It is true, they say, it is a wild nutmeg, that the mace is less florid, and the taste of the nut itself more pungent, though larger and fairer to the eye than the spice of the same kind brought by them from the East Indies. The cinnamon tree grows likewise in this island, though the bark is said to have a taste of cloves as well as cinnamon. Here likewise grows the tree that produces the true *gum copal*, resembling that brought from the continent of America, and very different from what goes by the same name in the rest of the West India islands. All ground provisions are produced here in the utmost abundance, as well as in the highest perfection. There is likewise plenty of wild hogs and other animals, together with great quantities of fowl, and an amazing variety both of sea and river fish. In the time the Dutch were in possession of this island, which was not many years, they exported large quantities of tobacco, sugar, cassia, ginger, cinnamon, sassafras, gum copal, cocoa, rocou, indigo, and cotton; besides rich woods, materials for dying, drugs of different kinds, and several sorts of delicious sweetmeats. We shall here take

take the liberty of observing, that there is at least the highest probability of our being able to produce all the valuable spices of the East Indies in this island. Cinnamon is said to grow in some of the other West India islands, and general Codrington had once an intention to try how much it might be improved by a regular cultivation in his island of Barbuda. It is universally allowed, that the bark of what is called the wild cinnamon tree in Tobago is beyond comparison the best in all the West Indies, and even in its present state may be made an article of great value. The bark when cured with care differs from that in the East Indies, by being stronger and more acrid while it is fresh; and when it has been kept for some time it loses that pungency, and acquires the flavour of cloves. This is precisely the spice for which there is a very considerable sale at Lisbon, Paris, and over all Italy. This kind of spice is drawn principally from Brazil, and the Portugueze believe that their cinnamon trees were originally brought from Ceylon, while it was in their possession, but that through the alteration of soil and climate they are degenerated into this kind of spice, and this may very probably be true: however, from their size and number it seems to admit of no doubt, that the common trees actually growing in Tobago are the natural production of that island, and the point with us is to know what improvement may be made with respect to these. The nutmeg tree, as well as the cinnamon, is a native of this island: we cannot doubt of the fact, that is, of the nutmeg's growing here; because we find it asserted in a book addressed to M. de Beveren, then governor of Tobago. A man who had invented a falsehood would hardly have had the boldness to repeat it, not only to a respectable person, but to the person in the world who must have the clearest knowledge of its being a falsehood. The nutmeg tree that naturally grows in Tobago, is in all probability as true, and may, by due care and pains, be rendered as valuable a nutmeg as those that grow any where else; for the fact really is, that wherever there are nutmegs, there are wild nutmegs, or, as some style them, mountain nutmegs, which are longer and larger, but much inferior in the flavour to the true nutmeg, and are very liable to be worm-eaten; the point is to know how these defects may be remedied, or, in other words, wherein the difference consists between the wild,

taste-

tasteless, and useless nutmeg, and that which is true, aromatic, and of course a valuable spice *.

This idea, with other arguments to inforce it, too cogent to be overturned, are to be met with in the same work, which it must be confessed by every one is very well reflected, and drawn up with much candour and judgment: but unfortunately for the interests of this country, they have met with no more attention than if the author had wrote concerning raising spices in the moon: it is near ten years since he composed his treatise, yet has not there been the least step taken towards making the experiment, though nothing can be more obvious than the design, nor more easy than the execution, of taking plants wild from the forest, and trying what change a regular cultivation will make in their flavour and nature. Our ministers have attended enough to *selling* the lands in these ceded islands, but as to the national improvement of them, they have neither thought nor cared about it. Very much is it to be regretted, that something at the public expence has not been done towards ascertain-

---

* *Considerations on the Sugar Trade.*

ing the degree of improvement which the native productions of these islands are capable of receiving. A very small public plantation for this purpose, under the conduct of an able botanist, would be sufficient for the experiment; nor can I see any good objections to such a scheme, upon the score of an expence which could hardly amount to more than a few hundred pounds a year.

Dropping the idea of improvements, which we may be certain will, for want of public virtue, never be executed, it remains for us to remark, that the ceded islands of St. Vincent, Dominica, Granada, and Tobago, are among the few principal acquisitions made by the late glorious war. Before the successes of that war took place, it was a common complaint in our islands that good sugar-land was so scarce, that the product of that commodity was entirely at a stand, while our rivals, the French, were making an amazing progress, owing to the great plenty of excellent land at their command: but the acquisition of these islands has at least lifted us from that stagnant situation, in which nothing but a decline could be expected; the purchase of land in these territories, and their cultivation, has animated our people since the last peace, and given

given them some of that activity which ever attends advance: in commerce and politics no enemy is more to be dreaded than standing still. Had we not secured these islands, our ruin in the West Indies must soon have followed, without the greatest dexterity of management, for France has made a much greater acquisition by gaining the Spanish half of Hispaniola in exchange for Louisiana; which is such an acquisition of valuable territory in the West Indies, as we can never hope again to make.

But while our rivals have such an advantage of territory, be it our aim to gain the ascendancy in industry; and that is principally to be done in the quick and thorough cultivation of these islands. Public arrangements ought to co-operate with private endeavours; encouragement should be given to settlers to plant those parts of the island which do not sell, which will of course be all the parts that do not possess every requisite for cane-grounds; but the climate is highly propitious to commodities as valuable as sugar: encouragement should be given to such settlers to go upon coffee, indigo, cocoa, cotton, cochineal, and other articles, so that every part of the islands, except those which it would be proper to leave in wood from ruggedness of situation, might be brought into some kind or other of profitable culture. With respect to spices, which certainly our India company might long ago have secured in some of their settlements, small plantations, of the native growths, should be made, in spots selected for that purpose, to see what perfection culture would bring them to; we should probably, by this means, gain at least some articles that would be useful and profitable in certain branches of our commerce. The expence would be small, the benefit might be great.

CHAP.

CHAP. XXXIII.

BAHAMA ISLANDS.

PROVIDENCE.

Climate — Soil—Productions—Observations on their neglected state—Proposals for their improvement.

THE Lucayos, or Bahama islands, are some hundreds in number, some of them many miles in length, and others little better than rocks or knoles rising above the water, which render navigation among them remarkably dangerous. They are seated in the finest climate of the world, between 21 and 27 deg. north latitude, which, though very hot on the continent, is in these islands but another word for an almost perpetual spring. The isle of Bahama is in lat. 26 deg. 30 min. being about 50 miles long, but very narrow. Providence is in 25 deg. it is 28 miles long, and 11 broad. Some of them are of much larger sizes than these, but not above three or four inhabited: Providence is the seat of government. In 1763, the imports to Great Britain were above four thousand pounds from Providence.

    I before remarked, that the climate is excellent in most of them; of this I have been assured by a gentleman who spent some time among them during the late war: he added, that the heats were temperated in the very hottest months by the sea breezes, and the number of the islands surrounding, gave them more than an equivalent to the land-breeze, by generally fanning them with eddies and gales of wind. Nothing of that suffocating heat which renders the West Indies so pernicious to European constitutions; and which strictly confines the inhabitants to their houses during the best part of the day; on the contrary, in July and August you may be out about any kind of rural sports or business without the least inconvenience. The healthiness of the islands is owing greatly to the dryness of their soil: there is not a swamp, a marsh, or a bog in any one that has been examined; they are high, dry, hilly, or rocky spots admirably watered with streams, being in the exemption from bad water, and in the possession of good, equal to any country in the known world.

While

While the heats in summer are so little oppressive, the spring is a season too delicious to admit description, and the winter is entirely free from snow or frost; the tenderest fruits of the West Indies flourish throughout them, and are of flavour equal to what is tasted in much hotter climates. The uncommon healthiness of the few inhabitants, proves how just this representation of the climate is.

Respecting the soil, it is in most of the larger islands various, but every where excellent. It consists generally of a loamy sand, in some places mixed with flints, and in others free from them: very considerable tracts are of a black rich mould, light, but of a putrid appearance, and of a good depth; this is not found only in the vallies, but along the slopes of the hills to a great tract of country through many of the islands. The extraordinary growth to which all vegetables, cultivated and spontaneous, arrive, is proof sufficient of the great fertility of this land. Among its productions are to be reckoned sugar, cotton, indigo of a remarkable fine quality, cocoa, ginger, pimento, wild cinnamon, pine apples, guavas, bananas, plantains, oranges, lemons, citrons, &c. these valuable articles are

are either wild, or cultivated in gardens; for the quantity in regular culture by way of plantation is very small, as may be judged by the whole product of all the islands at the British market being under five thousand pounds, and in that small sum their cedar and other valuable timber make a considerable portion.

If the fineness of the climate, and the richness of the soil be considered, it will appear self-evident, that every article usually cultivated in our West India isles, might with a certainty of success be raised here. Is it not therefore astonishing that they should be left in so neglected a state? That so few enterprising minds should be found to undertake plantations in them: tracts of land might here be chosen and had for no other expence than paying the usual fees of office; whereas 60l. per acre for land not better, is a common price in our sugar islands. That commodity might beyond all doubt be cultivated to no small advantage, for it thrives luxuriantly in much more northerly climates; and if the advantage of plenty of land, with all sorts of lumber on the spot, with a profusion of provisions of all kinds, both for the slaves and cattle of a plantation; if these circumstances

stances are considered, with the difference of having the land almost for nothing, or paying 60l. an acre for it—if these points are considered, it will be sufficiently plain, that considerable estates might be made by sugar-planting in these islands, as it is most certain that less crops than the produce of Jamaica and Barbadoes would pay better interest for a capital here, than large ones there, all expences carried to account.

But supposing that equal profit by sugar could not be made, which is much more than there is any necessity to grant, why should they not be applied to indigo, cotton, vines, tobacco, &c. In these articles there has never been a doubt of the climate being hot enough—nor can any person doubt but they would yield larger crops than are gained of them on the continent. And a beneficial culture of these commodities, in such of the islands as are capable of cultivation, would bring into this nation an annual profit of one or two hundred thousand pounds a year, without reckoning any thing for sugar: but if the most was made of them that they are capable of, knowing people well acquaintied with them, have thought they would be worth half a million

lion a year to Britain; inftead of producing not five thoufand pounds.

 The navigation, I am fenfible, of thefe iflands has always been reckoned very hazardous; but this notion muft not be adopted in general; when fhips have been driven in ftorms among their rocks and fhoals, feveral have been wrecked, but as to thofe that have fteered regularly thither as their courfe, the navigation has never proved dangerous: there is a regular communication open by fhips often paffing to and fro between Providence and Charles Town in Carolina, Philadelphia, &c. and alfo to the Leeward Iflands, not to fpeak of thofe which pafs between England and that ifland. And if the navigation is frequented for the fmall concerns of thefe iflands at prefent, and the few commodities of value they export, furely by a parity of reafoning we may fuppofe, that if more valuable products were raifed, and in much greater abundance, the navigation would not then be objected to: if it is fufficiently fafe to induce fhipping now to frequent it, moft certainly they would then. Nor fhould I omit to remark, that the inhabitants on the few iflands that are at all peopled, are the moft dextrous feamen in all America;

America; one principal branch of their employment is building sloops and other small vessels, with which they carry on a traffic between the northern colonies and the sugar islands, and export their own provisions in tolerable quantities to those islands; this makes them able navigators, and gives plenty of pilots for most of the passages and channels of their own Archipelago.

But there is another view in which these islands may be considered, which though not essential, yet deserves mention: it is that of affording perhaps the most agreeable and eligible retreat for men whose active or variegated lives have taken off that relish for the world which once actuated them; and to whom nothing appears with such charms as a prospect of a safe, easy, and agreeable retreat. Or to men who from failures, losses, disappointments, or a general want of income for living agreeably in a wealthy, luxurious, and expensive country, are desirous of spending, at least, some years of their life in a retirement, where their little fortunes may be sufficient for providing them with such enjoyments as their own country denies them: to any such, these islands could hardly appear in any other light but that of a paradise upon earth, which will plainly appear, from considering them with this view.

In the first place, here is an air and climate perfectly unexceptionable, as healthy to an European constitution as almost any other part of America; where the heats are never excessive, and where severe cold was never known: a clear serene sky, and an atmosphere free from every species of damps and fogs; a soil as fertile as any in the world in the production of all the articles that form the necessaries and superfluities of life, from bread to pine-apples, and that in a profusion which scarcely any other country experiences. In addition to these circumstances, here is further to be met with a plenty as remarkable of both sea and river fish, with various sorts of wild fowl and game: timber in every island for all the purposes of building whether houses, or sloops and boats. And in point of agreeableness, many of the islands abound in situations which are equally pleasing and romantic. There are in Mogane and some others of them the finest slopes of country that can be imagined. A wave of gentle but varied declivities from the tops

tops of very high hills, shelving down to a bold sea-shore; in some places spread with open lawn, in others scattered with open groves of tall trees, rivers winding in slopes, and in other places falling down the hills in cascades, the whole bounded generally by thick woods: some of these scenes take in the space of three, four, or six hundred acres, and have from the shipping the noblest effect imaginable.

Where now can such persons as I have mentioned, find a more eligible retreat than in such scenes as these! Much more so than the Bermudas Islands, where there is a confined society, which in the nature of things must be full of all the jars and bickerings of the world; and where the people are in too low a sphere of life to afford conversation pleasing or satisfactory to a man of any ideas. But the Bahamas are so circumstanced, that a man may live in just that degree of retirement he likes—that is, he may live entirely to himself, and come again into the world whenever he wishes for it.

IMPORTANCE
OF THE
AMERICAN COLONIES
TO
BRITAIN.

CHAP. XXXIV.

Principles upon which colonies are established—How far answered by those of Britain—Wherein their importance consists—Depends on climate—Observations.

IN conducting the reader the tour of all our colonies, I have laid before him every circumstance that was necessary for giving a complete idea of their agriculture; little has been said of their commerce or of their manufactures, because it was conceived, that it is upon the culture of their lands that the interest of this country in America chiefly depends; and because the channels through which my intelligence came,

came, principally afforded communications relative to agriculture. Upon the general importance of the colonies there has been much wrote, and by able pens; but from the extravagance to which certain arguments have been carried of late, we may reasonably conclude, that clear ideas are not yet entertained, not so much upon the importance in general, as the points upon which that importance principally depends. A very little discrimination is sufficient to convince us, that however well our best writers agree in that general circumstance, they are far from attributing effects to the same causes. What I shall chiefly attend to therefore in this chapter, will be to point out in what manner Britain reaps such great advantages by her colonies—in what degree it depends on their agriculture —what variations there are in husbandry, which are attended with corresponding variations in the interest of the mother-country. In making this enquiry, I shall be naturally led to clear up some apparent difficulties, which the reader might remark in his progress through the preceding pages.

There are three grand reasons for a country's planting colonies. *First*, affording a *national* retreat to such persons as will emigrate. *Secondly*, affording a retreat to the emigrants of foreign countries. *Thirdly*, raising the productions of climates different from their own, and thereby saving the purchase of such productions.

As to the first reason, every one must know that there is a certain degree of emigration at all times going on from all nations; necessity or private inclination will carry many people from one country to another, and very many of the number are indifferent where they go, provided it is from home—or to a country in which they can maintain themselves better than at home; if they go from Britain to France or Spain, those countries are proportionably strengthened, and we are weakened; it is therefore of particular importance to provide a colony for such persons, that they may not, by their emigration, add to the population of an enemy's country, or that of a rival. For the same reason that makes this rule of conduct adviseable, it is also to be wished, that the emigrants from our enemies and rivals may make choice of our colonies, by which means, at the same time that they weaken them, they strengthen us. From the many favours nature has showered

showered down upon some of our American settlements, we see them resorted to by numbers of French, Dutch, Germans, Danes, Swedes, and Switzers, adding thereby greatly to the populousness of the country, and enriching Britain by their labour. The third reason for forming colonies is no less cogent; countries in a northern latitude, like Britain, cannot raise either sugar, tea, coffee, wine, silk, tobacco, indigo, cochineal, and many other articles; nor can their own territories yield a sufficiency of hemp, flax, iron, timber, &c. all such commodities must therefore be purchased in the way of trade from other nations; but if the import is large, the country is under a necessity of exporting other commodities or manufactures in great quantities, or a considerable balance must be paid in bullion, to the impoverishment of the country: and in proportion to the import of such commodities, is the industry and wealth of other nations increased at the expence of Britain. Hence the value of colonies that will provide us with such commodities, which spares our taking them from foreign nations, which sell them to us not for bullion but for manufactures; and whose increase in people and wealth is so much added to the scale of Britain, instead of that material deduction which the increase of some of our neighbours makes from us. This is so evident, that it can scarcely be contradicted with propriety.

Here therefore we deduce, that the population of the colonies is an increasing weight in the scale of Britain, and that their producing those commodities which the climate of Britain refuses, or which we cannot raise in sufficient quantity, is an advantage of the first magnitude. The excess to which the first may be carried in time, will be more properly examined, when I come to consider the probability of their independance.

In the production of such staples as Britain cannot produce herself, there are some circumstances which demand distinctions; for the policy of colonization is one of the most curious speculations that can be made in general politics. When the products are raised, should they be brought to Britain in British or American vessels? Should the same products be sold to other nations, and in what manner? Should the colonies pursue other employments, such as commerce, manufactures, or fisheries? How are they to be restrained? And in these queries

ries it is not to be supposed merely what a mother-country would wish for—but what she would command, from the nature of her superiority.

A wide field for discussion here opens itself, but having been so much discussed by others, the less will suffice from me.

Two circumstances require equal attention; first, preserving the natural and political rights of the Americans; and secondly, the interest of Britain: it is not necessary that either should be sacrificed to the other, but then a sensible and attentive conduct is essential: things must not be left to their own progress, but thrown by artificial means into that train which is necessary for both. Colonies may naturally think themselves entitled to the common privileges of raising what commodities they please—selling them to whom they please—navigating their vessels how and where they please—and, in a word, acting to all purposes as a mother-country. But on the other hand, if all this is indulged, instead of being colonies they are independant states, and a country can never have any interest in planting and supporting such.

That a strong distinction must be made here is evidently necessary: the mother-country discovers, founds, peoples, and supports the people for some ages; does not this lay them under an obligation different from what is experienced by any original and independant people? Does it not, upon the very face of it, imply a dependance, or an agreement to certain conditions? Is it to be supposed, that any people would plant colonies with any other idea? And is it not clear that the people who go to them do in that action, and in accepting the protection of the mother-country, tacitly acknowledge and agree to a submission to those reciprocal terms of agreement which are supposed to bind them? These *supposed* terms (for no absolute expression can be given to so uncertain an idea) are a general obedience to the acts of the British legislature, when legally, and according to the laws of nations, exerted. In the establishment and progress of all our colonies they invariably obeyed the authority of the British parliament, and in many instances even that of the crown; and what is of consequence, they received perpetual accessions of new settlers during the whole period of their submission to such authority. All this proves sufficiently, that the mother-country has an undoubted right so to regulate

the

he pursuits of the colonies, as to render them consistent with her own interest.

It has been found, for instance, necessary to prevent the colonies from trading immediately with foreign nations; a point of policy necessary in the management of all the colonies which the European nations have settled in America; for if this was allowed, they would to all useful purposes be the colonies of other powers as much as of our own. It has also been enacted, that no law passed in the American assemblies shall have force till assented to by king and council in England. Various other instances might be given, but these are sufficient to shew a restraining and superior power. And in the exertions of this power we see nothing to shock the political liberty and freedom of the colonists, any more than in distant countries of England being governed by laws passed at Westminster, and to which perhaps not a five hundredth part of the inhabitants ever gave a direct or virtual assent.

Having premised these circumstances, which prove that the mother country had a right, and must always enjoy it, of regulating the pursuits of the colonies, so as to turn them to their own advantage, it remains

mains to be confidered how far this conduct has been purfued by Britain, in which enquiry will be feen thofe errors which have brought on the differences that have lately happened between her and her American plantations.

I before obferved, that one great benefit refulting from colonies was the production of fuch commodities as the climate of the mother-country will not yield; this advantage Britain has experienced in an high degree. Her iflands in the Weft Indies produce that great modern luxury, fugar, in larger quantities than fhe can confume; fo that after fatisfying her own confumption, there remains a furplus which is re-exported to other nations of Europe that have not fugar iflands. We have fhewn in the preceding pages what a confiderable fum this total amount of fugar, &c. is, which, being in this age a neceffary of life, muft have been bought of France, had we not poffeffed our Weft India iflands. The amount of thefe commodities is between two and three millions fterling, a fum fufficient to drain any nation, and would at this day, while the trade of the kingdom is in a moft flourifhing fituation, give fuch a balance againft her,

her, as to bring on every evil that can accrue from the impoverishment of a people.

If it be said that the West Indies and England are not the same country, and that these commodities, at least as much of them as are consumed, cost the nation as much as if bought of foreigners, I reply, that supposing this was true, which is not the case, still there is this essential difference, that in the transaction with our own islands we pay in manufactures, but in our transaction with a foreign country, we must pay in whatever the balance of the commerce between the two nations is paid in, which, with such a vast import added, would certainly be bullion. We already pay a considerable annual balance to France; but what would that balance be if our import of West India commodities was added to it? Importation of any thing, and in almost any quantity, is harmless, or perhaps beneficial, as long as paid for with manufactures; for such importation is then the means of feeding our poor, and supporting our population. But this is not the only advantage resulting from our islands: in the cultivation and sale of the commodity, there is a great profit made by the planter, as we every day

see

see by the large estates made in that part of the world: all these estates come at last to Britain—every great fortune made enables the possessor to come over and live here, and he leaves his plantation to overseers. The overseers in their turn make fortunes, and do the same; and fresh overseers are left for the same purpose: but the end of the whole is the same, all the money that is made in considerable sums is sure to send its owners to England. What the amount of such incomes spent by absentees is, cannot be discovered, but every one's knowledge must tell him that it must be very considerable. This circumstance is clear profit, from having sugar colonies of our own, instead of buying our sugar, &c. from France or other countries.

Nor is the employment of shipping and seamen to be forgotten, which are of the very first importance to a maritime and commercial power: the navigation to the West Indies breeds and employs many seamen, all of which would be lost to the nation, if she was to lose her sugar colonies; or, what would be worse than lost, they might be added to the navigation of France and other countries, than which nothing could be more highly detrimental. The freight

freight alone of our West India staples amounts to above half a million sterling, whereas the share we should have in the freight of the same commodities from European countries would be very insignificant in its amount.

I have entered particularly into this enquiry concerning the sugar colonies, because they are more immediately applicable to every circumstance of the argument than most of our other settlements: and the instance is strong to shew us the great importance of planting colonies in such climates as produce commodities totally different from those of the mother-country; in a luxurious age the products of one zone are necessaries of life in another; in order therefore to have as many commodities as possible, without purchasing them of foreign nations, the mother-country should be in one zone and the colonies in another, which is the case with Britain and her West India islands. It is these principles which have proved so fortunate in the colonization we have carried on in this part of the world; and whether we consider wealth, employment of our poor, of our seamen, shipping, and all the attendants of navigation, we must decide that
our

our West India islands are in every respect as valuable settlements as any the world can boast. France possesses others in the same region, which are superior only in proportion as they are superior in numbers and quantity; the qualities of one are equal to those of the other.

While we reap such immense advantages from these islands, it is necessary to observe two circumstances, first, that they are gained without laying any violence or constraint upon them, which is contrary to the common principles of all colonies, or the natural liberties and rights of mankind; and secondly, that the benefits we receive from them are greatly owing to their attending to agriculture alone. The first shews, that the national advantage made by colonies does not result from opppression, but from a fair communication of reciprocal benefits. On the second I must observe, that it is the case to a very extraordinary degree: the West India islands are, I apprehend, more free from manufactures than any other territories in the world. In all our continental plantations there are either manufactories or numerous families who spin, weave, and do other works of *manufacture* for the cloathing or answering other wants

wants of themselves or a part of themselves. But in the islands there is hardly to be found a man, woman, or child, that has a single article of dress, furniture, or implement of business, but what is imported: this shews that husbandry is the most profitable employment they can follow. While a man was taken up in weaving a piece of cloth, or making hose or any other manufacture which brought him in five pounds for his labour, he would, in working upon the land, or at those trades dependant on the land, earn three times that sum; from whence it follows, that manufactures can never be introduced into such a country, since, in order to make them, such wages must be given as would render the fabric vastly dearer than the same made in England, with all the additional charges of sending it to the West Indies, which would bring ruin to all such undertakings. Neither do the inhabitants of these islands apply themselves to commerce, except it be to the illicit trade with the Spaniards, in which very great profits are made; and even in this many more North American vessels are found than West Indian, for it much deserves attention, that these islands possess very few ships, or, more properly speak-

speaking, scarcely any; their trade is carried on in North American or British vessels—even when the planters turn merchants, as most of them do, in shipping their own products, still they do it all in vessels belonging to other people. All this is owing to the profit of their business; when their husbandry is so beneficial, as to pay, we will suppose, 25, 30, or 35 per cent. it would ill answer to have money in shipping at 8 or 10 per cent.

Here therefore is an example of colonies going of themselves into the pursuit which the mother-country has the greatest reason to approve and promote: every circumstance attending colonization in the West Indies is precisely in the train best calculated for the interest of Britain, and at the same time for the profit of the planters. This is not the case with all our colonies; to what therefore is it owing here? The answer to this is ready enough; it is owing to *the profit of their husbandry.* Every people will give their application to that branch of industry which they find most advantageous; if the soil and climate of a colony are such as will produce *valuable* commodities, it is to the production of such commodities they will apply. Why is not Barbadoes filled with mer-

merchants, fishermen, manufactures, and farmers, like New England? Because planting sugar is there a more profitable employment. Why is not New England filled with planters? Because trade, fishing, manufacturing, and farming, are more profitable employments. This distinction is that of climate, and it gives a lesson of all others the most important in the politics of colonization, which is to plant them in climates the reverse of the mother-country. This is the principle upon which depends the immense consequence of our West Indian possessions. Britain and those islands are similar in none of their products: the latter wants every thing produced by the former; the former wants every thing produced by the latter; thus it is impossible the one should ever rival the other, as the communication between them consists of a regular exchange of good offices, the one yields upon the balance profit to the other; protection and a ready market are dispensed in return.

If from the West Indies we proceed northward to the southern continental colonies, we shall find as we go continued reasons to shew the great importance of colonies to Britain: by that title I mean the tlements to the south of the tobacco colonies; these produce rice, indigo, cotton, silk, wine, and other commodities which are of great value in a British market, and which Britain cannot produce herself: the same reasons that make the sugar colonies of so much value to us, render these the same; and though some writers have calculated that these settlements are not so valuable as the islands proportioned to the numbers of their people, yet we are to remember, that this is not owing to a want of value in their products, (some of which, silk and indigo, are far more costly than sugar), but to the country being more agreeable and healthy to live in, which induces many persons to reside in their back parts, and cultivate common provisions to supply the rest with—and also to the ease with which any man who has five or ten pounds, may get a grant of land, build a hut, buy a cow or two, and turn farmer; such people, though they reckon in the numbers of the province, produce perhaps none of the staples of it: whereas, if only those were reckoned who are employed on the staples and the trades dependant, they would be found to raise as great an amount per head as the planters of the sugar colonies.

nies. This circumstance does not act in the islands from two causes, first the want of land, which is so far from being given to whoever will have it, that it is sold at considerable prices;—secondly, the unwholesomeness of the climate, which is in general such, that no person would chuse to make it their residence for small profits, or with any other view than to make money enough to be able to live elsewhere. These circumstances cannot but have the effect of fixing far more people in the continental colonies, proportioned to the production of staples, than in the West Indies.

This kingdom enjoys a very considerable trade by means of these colonies; out of above an hundred thousand barrels of rice which they export, we do not consume ourselves above four or five thousand; the rest goes to Spain, Portugal, Germany, Holland, and the North. Indigo is an article of the first consequence to our manufactures, silk is the same, raw hides the same; so that these commodities are in fact equally valuable to us with sugar: they are not bought with money, but with manufactures; the navigation occasioned by them is all our own, so that they add to our strength and wealth in the same manner as sugar, cocoa, coffee, ginger, &c. The southern colonies have no manufactures among them, they are without fisheries, and their commerce consists in nothing but sending lumber to the West Indies, and shipping their staples for a British market in British bottoms.

Objections indeed would have been raised against the production of rice, upon the principle of its being a grain, which in the European markets rivals the exportation of British corn. This has an appearance of truth, and in some years in a small degree may be so: but it is not to be supposed, that if we had sold no rice, we should have added a proportional quantity to the export of corn: nothing can be farther from truth. Rice is purchased by very many people, who would not lay the money out in corn if they could not get the rice: it is used for soup and other different purposes from corn; and if consumed to save wheat by some, it may be a matter of choice rather than œconomy. Nor should we forget that our corn exportation is quite another thing from the export of rice from Carolina, it is uncertain, depends upon the crop; prohibitions have of late been common

mon and continual; and in several years we have imported instead of exported: now it would certainly have been very absurd to have restrained or wished to have restrained the culture of rice, because it is possible that it may rival us to the amount of two or three thousand pounds in four or five hundred thousand pounds worth that is sold. Besides, the export of rice is regular; it is a grain that depends very little on the seasons, and being made not for the consumption of the country where grown, but in order all to be exported, the money gained by the trade comes as regularly as the year; and is, in a word, the very contrary of our corn trade for some years past. For these reasons we may determine rice to be a very proper staple for a colony, and may look on its increase of culture with satisfaction, instead of being jealous of it. If it increases in future, as it has done of late years, it will soon bring more money into the kingdom than any other commodity.

If we advance yet farther northward, and take in the tobacco colonies, those of Virginia and Maryland, we shall find the same reasons to congratulate ourselves upon the great value they are of. Tobacco is the grand

grand staple of these settlements, a staple as proper as possible for a colony, and than which none is more valuable to this kingdom. Out of 96,000 hogsheads made, only 13,500 are consumed in Britain, and the duty alone of these is 26 l. 1 s. per hogshead, or 351,675 l. The rest is re-exported to the other parts of Europe, paying also a duty, though not so heavy, and bringing a flood of wealth into this kingdom.

Every circumstance that can concur to render a colony valuable to a mother-country, unites in this product, tobacco. Much the larger part of it is consumed by foreign nations—it could not be profitably raised in Britain—it is a bulky commodity, which employs many ships and seamen—those ships are all our own, and the seamen belonging to the ports of Britain—it is so profitable an article of husbandry, as to preclude all other employments like sugar, as long as good land is to be had to plant. All these circumstances are of vast importance, and should make us as solicitous to increase and improve the tobacco culture, as any other article of our American produce.

The

The excellency of this staple is seen in its enabling the planter to buy every necessary of life except food, and without his attending to any other object. These colonies, so far from rivalling us in fisheries, manufactories, or commerce, have none of the three among them, insomuch that people have found so little profit in herding together, that there has never yet arose a single town of any consequence in either Maryland or Virginia; a strong proof of the advantage they find in spreading over the country as planters, rather than fixing in towns as merchants and manufacturers. These colonies, from the health and fertility of the climate and soil, are grown very populous, and in proportion as their numbers have increased, there has not been an increase of fresh land for their tobacco planting: this has been owing, first, to the confinement which the war gave their settlements, and afterwards to the extreme ill-judged proclamation of 1763, which forbid all settlements beyond the rivers which fall into the Atlantic ocean: this has driven many of their people to common husbandry, to which the soil and climate are equally well adapted. The consequence of this was, that when the export of tobacco is divided among the population of the provinces, the people seem to earn by it but a small sum, compared to those of the islands and the southern colonies. But we are not from thence to conclude that the staple is deficient in value; on the contrary, I am of opinion, that if the amount of it was divided only among the people actually employed by it, and depending on it, it would then be found more valuable even than sugar, or at least as valuable. A part of the population applying, for want of fresh land, to the culture of wheat and provisions, is no fault in tobacco.

But of as great importance as this plant is, yet we are to remember, that it is not the only staple of this colony; it has some other very promising ones. £.

Hemp, 1000 tons, 21l.	21,000
30 sail of ships,	30,000
Masts, planks, &c.	55,000
Iron,	35,000
Skins,	25,000
Flax-seed,	14,000
Ginseng and drugs,	7,000
	£. 187,000

Besides

Besides 4000 tons more of hemp worked into the uses of their ships, &c. all these articles are true staples, being such as Britain either buys of foreign countries, or can sell to them in any quantities: they are articles also which promise a considerable increase, and which may be carried to a height as the population of these provinces increase, which, with the help of silk and wine, may bye-and-bye be as valuable as tobacco.

It may not be improper here to review the staples of these colonies, the southern ones, and the islands, as they all unite in the circumstance of having such valuable staples as render them in every respect highly valuable to Great Britain, and more so than other settlements more to the north can prove. The commodities chiefly produced in all our settlements, from Maryland to Grenada, are such as we cannot have at home, of which we consume great quantities, which must be purchased of foreigners, and perhaps of enemies, if we had not colonies that produced them. This advantage renders the consumption of those commodities, not to speak of the re-exportation of many, a benefit to the kingdom rather than an evil; for as the purchase

chase is made with our manufactures, the wealthy part of the nation, in proportion as they consume American luxuries, find employment for their poor neighbours; instead of which, if we had no colonies, the rental of their estates would go for the employment of poor Frenchmen and Germans; the immense difference of which is obvious at first sight. A late writer, from whom however I have had reason in the preceding pages to differ in certain articles, gives the following table of the tobacco and southern colonies.

	Ships.	Seamen.
Virginia and Maryland,	330	3,960
North Carolina,	34	408
South Carolina,	140	1,680
Georgia,	24	240
St. Augustine,	2	24
Pensacola,	10	120
	*540	6,432
Sugar islands, †		3,600
		10,032

	Exports from Britain.	Exports from Colonies.
Virginia and Maryland,	865,000	1,040,000
North Carolina,	18,000	68,350
Carried over,	883,000	1,108,350

* *American Traveller.*
† *Editor of Du Pratz.*

Brought forward,	883,0000	1,108,350
South Carolina,	365,000	395,666
Georgia,	49,000	74,200
St. Auguftine,	7,000	
Penfacola,	97,000	63,000
	*1,401,000	1,641,216
Weft Indies, †		2,702,060
		4,343,276

Thefe accounts are not the neweft, and I have corrected fome of the particulars from whence they are drawn, elfewhere, as I obferved before; the real totals at prefent, could they be all known, probably would not be found lefs than 13,000 feamen, 650 fhips, and colony exports of 5,000,000 l. but whether fomething more, or fomething lefs, the conclufions to be drawn are the fame: the poffeffion of colonies that produce ftaples which caufe fuch a prodigious commerce of the moft advantageous fort in the world; which is entirely carried on in our own products and manufactures, the balance of which is ours—the profit of which, on both fides, is ours—the fhips ours—the feamen ours—the freight ours—a flourifhing revenue

---

* *American Traveller.*
† *Political Effays.*

raifed

raised on them, ours—the population of the countries which support this trade, of our brethren and subjects of the same crown: when all these circumstances are considered, they will be found to involve a magnitude of interests which have long supported the greatness of Britain; which now is the most firm support of it; and which, by a prudent and political conduct in future, can hardly fail of being an increasing and improving support.

These therefore are colonies that it much behoves this country to give every degree of encouragement to that it is possible they should receive; for by encouraging them, she in fact encourages herself. I shall hereafter endeavour to shew, wherein such encouragement ought to consist: but I shall at present observe, that we ought to be very tender of increasing one branch of their value to us, that of *duties*, for therein we cramp instead of extending their products. Upon tobacco the duties are near three times the value, which is carrying that taxation to a degree which hardly any other commodity knows. Cases may happen which may make it very adviseable to lower such burthens, though I believe not unless our government is very ill advised in American affairs: but if (which however is hardly to be expected) the governments of those countries which produce either at home or in colonies the same commodities should take political steps for greatly encouraging such products, such a rivalship would render counter operations necessary; in which that of lowering duties would be found essential.

As to the northern colonies, all to the north of the tobacco ones may with propriety be classed together, since neither Pensylvania, New Jersey, New England, Nova Scotia, nor Canada, have any staple product of agriculture; the consequence of which is their flying to all other employments; the culture of the soil is common husbandry, like that of Britain herself; the employment of their towns, which are numerous and large, is manufactures, commerce, and fisheries. It is impossible they should be so employed, and at the same time be the occasion of Britain's prosperity, like the colonies to the south. But some writers have carried this deficiency of the northern colonies too far, in allowing under 100,000 l. for all their staples: that this matter may be set in a clear light, I shall transcribe here the totals of several articles before inserted in the tables of their exports, by extracting those articles which may be called staples.

		£.	
Skins,	Hudson's Bay,	29,340	
	Canada,	76,000	
	New York,	35,000	
	Pensylvania,	50,000	
			190,340
Ginseng and drugs,	Canada,		3,000
Timber,	Canada,	11,000	
	Nova Scotia,	4,000	
	New England,	75,000	
	New York,	25,000	
	Pensylvania,	35,000	
			150,000
Ships,	New England 70	49,000	
	New York 20	14,000	
	Pensylvania 25	17,500	
			80,500
Pitch, &c.	New England,	- -	600
Pot-ash,	New England,	35,000	
	New York,	14,000	
			49,000
Flax seed,	New York,	14,000	
	Pensylvania,	30,000	
			44,000
Copper and iron,	New York,	20,000	
	Pensylvania,	35,000	
			55,000
	Total,	£.	572,440

The tobacco of Virginia alone amounts to more money than all these staples, of all these colonies which contain thrice the people of those to the south: but at the same

same time we must acknowledge these to be staples, to every intent and purpose, doubts have been conceived about timber and ship-building; but when it is considered that there is scarcely any commodity that Britain wants more, witness her imports from the Baltic, and building even men of war with fir, there will not be found any reasons for rejecting them.

The reader will at once recollect that the exports of these colonies amount to far greater sums in fish, oil, wheat, &c. but these are certainly to be rejected, because in proportion as they increase the interest of Britain declines. The most capital article is that of fish, both cod and whale, and therefore I shall give it the first examination; as it includes more particularly their great navigation—commerce with foreign nations—and the employment of seamen; all which being of the greatest importance to Britain, we ought to enquire whether they are the same in the hands of the colonies. And this I shall do in the words of a late author, who has attended much to this subject.

We are told by Dr. Mitchel, that the British plantations maintain 45,000 seamen, and employ near 2000 sail of ships. Now as we have found the number which Britain *possesses* to be about 12,000, consequently their own amounts to about 33,000. A North American writer likewise calculates the ships at 2000. That these accounts are not exaggerated, there is some reason to believe from an assertion of another writer, who, speaking of the consequences of the regulations of the colonies in 1763, says that 20,000 seamen and fishermen were turned out of employment there. Now if 20,000 were at once *out* of employment, the total *in* as well as *out* cannot be less than 33,000, especially as the fisheries were not affected. And if we come to remark the sentiments of various writers upon *particular branches* of their trade, there will be more reasons equally strong for supposing this total not far from the reality. Gee, who wrote about 40 years ago, says, the vessels belonging to New England alone, employed in the fishery and coasting trade (without including that to Europe) amounted to 800. So prodigiously as they have increased since, the reader will easily believe them to be much more numerous of late years; and yet that number, at 22 men each, employed 17,600 seamen. To double the number, would

would bring it much nearer the truth at present. The fishery of the colonies, says Dr. Mitchel, is already much greater than that of Britain: the fishery of New England alone amounts to 255,000 l. a year, which is equal to the amount of the British fishery. And yet New York and Philadelphia, with many other places to the northward, have large shares of this fishery; so that the whole must make a very great amount.

Without turning to more authorities, (although a multitude might be produced) for proving a point which seems so strongly to prove itself, there will not be any danger, according to these several accounts, in determining the navigation *of the colonies* to employ 33,000 seamen; but left any objections unseen should arise, I shall call the number only 30,000. It may possibly be expected that I should enlarge upon the vast consequences of such a number of seamen to a maritime power, and especially after what one of the best of the North American writers has observed with a degree of rapture. "In another century the greatest number of Englishmen will be on this side the water. What an accession of power to the British empire, by *sea* as well as by land!

land! What increase of trade and navigation! What numbers of ships and seamen! We have been here but little more than 100 years, and yet the force of our privateers in the late war (1750) united, was greater both in men and guns than that of the whole British navy in queen Elizabeth's time." What therefore must they have been in the last war? But notwithstanding all this, I am very far from placing to the account of Britain one jot of all these fine doings. And very clear I am, that the employment of the 12,000 seamen first mentioned, is of twenty times the consequence to this country of all the 30,000 kept by the colonies themselves. The more this subject is enquired into, the more evidently and clearly will it appear, that the production of staple commodities is the *only* business proper for colonies: whatever else they go upon, it is absolutely impossible that they should by any employment whatever make up for the want of the one really necessary. For want of this capital foundation of a colony, our northern settlements, we have found, are full of farmers, manufacturers, merchants, fishermen, seamen;—but no planters. This is precisely the case with Britain herself; consequently a rival-a rivalry between them muſt inevitably take place. This in the article of the fiſheries we find fully taken place; for the northern colonies have nearly beaten us out of the Newfoundland fiſheries, that great nurſery of ſeamen! infomuch that the ſhare of New England alone exceeds that of Britain. Can any one think from hence, that the *trade* and *navigation* of our colonies are worth one groat to this nation?

There is not one branch of commerce carried on by theſe trading ſettlements but might juſt as well be in the hands of the inhabitants of this kingdom, the ſupplying the ſugar iſlands with lumber alone excepted, and that we have already ſeen is a trifle. Thus the trading part of the colonies rob this nation of the invaluable treaſure of 30,000 ſeamen, and all the profits of their employment; or in other words, the northern colonies, who contribute nothing either to our riches or our power, deprive us of more than twice the amount of all the navigation we enjoy in conſequence of the ſugar iſlands, the ſouthern, continental, and tobacco ſettlements! The freight of the ſtaples of thoſe ſetts of colonies bring us in upwards of a million ſterling; that is, the navigation of 12,000 ſeamen: according to which proportion we lose by the rivalry of the northern colonies in this single article TWO MILLIONS AND AN HALF sterling! The hackneyed argument which has been copied from writer to writer, that let the colonies get what they will, it all centers in Britain, will doubtless here be extended; and they will say, if the northern colonies get so much money, that money to them is the same as staples to the southern ones, and equally laid out in merchandize with Britain. But facts prove the very contrary: the consumption of British commodities in them I have shewed cannot be more than to the amount of 108,000 l. They export thither in staples to the amount of 98,000 l. now one of the warmest advocates above quoted asserts the fisheries of New England *alone* to be 255,000 l. according to this reasoning, they would purchase of us only for these two articles to the amount of 353,000, which being more than three times over false, sufficiently proves that they may acquire riches without expending them with Britain.

No one, who has enquired the least into the state of the colonies, can be ignorant that these northern commercial ones carry on a very considerable illicit trade. A late writer

writer says it amounted to a third of their actual imports. Now under the title of their imports is included *all* they receive from Britain and the West Indies, or in value to upwards of 917,000 l. a vast sum! and must in the nature of things be nearly so much taken out of the pockets of their mother country. Another writer lets us somewhat more into their illicit trade.—
" The colonies to the northward (of the tobacco ones) have very little direct trade with Great Britain; I mean they have nothing with which they can repay us for the commodities they draw from hence: they only trade with England circuitously; either through the West Indies, which is to us the most advantageous part of their trade, or through foreign European countries, which, however necessary, is a dangerous and suspicious channel. Our English ships meet others with the same commodities at the same markets; and if these markets happen to be overstocked, we interfere with and consequently hurt each other. But what is still more material, there is much reason to suspect that no small part of the benefit of our North American trade is by this means *lost to the mother-country, and passes to foreigners, and sometimes*

times to enemies. These northern provinces are in effect not subject to the act of navigation; because they do not trade in any of the commodities enumerated in that act. They are therefore neither obliged directly to bring their goods to England, nor when they have carried them to other countries, are they necessitated to take England in their way home. Whereas all the colonies which produce any of the enumerated commodities, under whatever relaxations, are always subject to one or other of these regulations. For instance, ships from Boston may carry fish, corn, and provisions to France and Italy, and return again directly to Boston, loaden with foreign commodities, subject to no other check, than what must be considered as none, that of a custom-house officer in their own colony *. These ships, however, carry out something else besides corn and fish; for the governor of Massachuset's Bay, in 1733, writes word to the Lords of Trade, that *vast quantities* of hats are exported from thence to Spain and Portugal: thus they carry out their own to

---

* *Examination of the Commercial Principles of the late Negociation.*

cramp

cramp our market, and bring home French goods to *enlarge* that of *our enemies* *. The general turn of reasoning through this passage is certainly just, though some particular sums are probably erroneous. The consumption of British manufactures in the northern colonies probably much exceeds 108,000l. but that they consume all they import, is most certainly contrary to every article of good intelligence that can be gained in the whole affair.

That fisheries and navigation are improper employments for colonies, and detrimental to the interests of the mother-country, appears clearly enough from hence; and I may add to these reasons, that the practice of the French, whose fishery employs 20,000 seamen, while ours maintains only 4000, proves strongly that *planted* settlements are by no means necessary for success in fishing. When they had Louisbourg, it was only a place of arms; a security to their fishery, and by no means a *colony*; and their fishery is now carried on in full perfection, without so much as that: thus no argument can be more false than that which pretends that our colonies have

---

* *Political Essays.*

not robbed Britain, but only created a new fishery from the advantageousness of their situation. We see the fishery of Britain is declined greatly, which, with the increase of that of New England, proves the fact sufficiently. We are told that of New England alone is greater than Britain's; suppose the seamen 5000; can any one imagine the employment of those men, with all the trades they set to work, not to be of the highest value to this kingdom, and the country that has gained them so far rivals and enemies? What advantage do we reap from New England equal to this single loss?

The second article which I was to consider, is that of corn and provisions, which are exported from all these northern colonies to the West Indies and to Europe. How far these are to be considered as staples, a short enquiry will shew. As to all that are sent to Europe, we may safely determine it to be as pernicious a trade as any the colonies can go into, since it is directly rivalling, and even destroying one of the most advantageous branches of the exports of Britain. American corn cannot come to an European market without doing mischief to the corn trade of England.

This

This trade is not like that of most other commodities, which are usually exported in certain quantities, and to certain markets: on the contrary, it is extremely uncertain in its destination, the quantity in demand depends on the accidents of crops, sometimes it is to one country, sometimes to another, and the circulation of the trade greatly depending on the surplus quantity which certain countries possess. Poland, England, and Barbary may be called the exporting countries; the latter from the uncertainty of its governments rarely makes the most of the fertility of its soil, proving but a weak rival to England: this leaves all the south of Europe open to the export of that country, and very advantageous the circumstance has been, as we have more than once experienced, both to Portugal, Spain, the south of France, and Naples. Let therefore any person judge of the propriety of introducing another rival into this trade, which is far more likely to drive us out of it, than all the others we can have in Europe. Wheat, for many years, sold at 20s. a quarter in America, which was their exporting price, the freight to Marseilles or Naples is 12s. more, the price therefore delivered has been 32s. a quar-

quarter; a price at which we have never yet fold in thofe markets, even with the affiftance of the bounty. If this does not fhew the great impropriety, not to ufe a harfher expreffion, of planting colonies in climates that will not produce ftaple commodities, furely nothing can. It may be faid, perhaps, that importation from thefe colonies, even to Britain herfelf, may be an advantageous meafure in dear years; but I cannot but confider fuch an idea as very fatal: it implies a dependence on America, which may grow into a neglect of our agriculture at home; than which a more fatal event can never happen. Britain fhould never look forward to fcarcities of corn; if fhe does, fhe will be fure to find them. Let her, on the contrary, have no other idea but that of exporting, which will be the means of always keeping it cheap, as we have found for near a century.

There is another evil attending this exportation of American corn to Europe; it is the largenefs of the market; while the North Americans were confined to the demand of the Weft Indies, they could look no farther, and raife no more wheat than fufficient for that demand; but having the European

European market to go to, increases this culture among them prodigiously: the consequence of which is, to draw them off from the culture of staples, and from those other professions which are more beneficial to the mother-country. If the demand for wheat was not large—and the farmers raising little more than sufficient for their families, they have no encouragement to extend their culture—and the profit on the husbandry is small, in this situation many farmers had great inducements to move to the southward, and turn planters; as many did. But when exportation finds a regular market for all they grow, in a country where land is so plentiful, it makes the common husbandry as profitable as planting, and instead of farmers turning planters, planters turn farmers, than which nothing can be more fatal to the interests of Britain.

In the second place, as to the supply of the West Indies, the same objections do not lie; for as the islands find planting too profitable to allow them to attend to common husbandry, there certainly can be no objection to the northern colonies answering the demand—any more than to their supplying them with lumber; but let

let me here make a remark, that I do not recollect ever hearing from any quarter, or reading in any of the numerous works that have been published on this subject. It is that Britain in good policy ought to have kept this supply entirely to herself, instead of the uncertain corn trade she has had with Europe; for this, I think, many reasons are to be given; the demand which there has been in Europe for British corn has never been regular; it has been on the contrary very uncertain; and even in years, when exportation has run very high, it has not been answerable to the surplus of our crop, as we may judge from the price at home continuing so low that the farmers could in several countries scarcely live. Now the supply of the West Indies is the most beneficial market that is known in the world; for it is perfectly regular, and absolutely to be depended upon. No where else are such considerable bodies of people as the inhabitants of those islands, to be found, that depend for their daily bread on importation, that attempt to raise scarce any thing that they eat: Britain therefore might have depended absolutely on this market; and the supply of it would have been more beneficial than the corn trade she

she has at fits and starts carried on in Europe: but the encouragement her agriculture would have received by this *regular* demand would have so animated it, that larger quantities of corn than ever would have been produced, and she would have found no difficulty in supplying the European demand also. This might have been done with great ease, by only laying a duty in the islands upon the import of all corn, except from Britain and Ireland: I do not think this would have been a severity to the islands, because there are many ports for exporting corn from Britain, and many corn merchants in every port; so that there would never have been any reason to fear a plentiful supply, and at a fair price—and if the rate at which the corn came to them was judged too high, the same bounty on the export, or even a larger, if necessary, than what is given at present, would have remedied the inconvenience. As to the distance and freight, we are certain they would have been no material objection, from what we know to be the case at present, which is the supply the islands at present receive from England of beans, and from Ireland of beef. If beans will answer

swer such a freight, most certainly wheat would.

Such a measure as this at present would be perhaps a dangerous one, because all sudden changes in matters of commerce are ever hazardous: but nothing would have been easier than to have established it before the exports from the northern colonies were so large, while the trade was low, and the supply not considerable; the measure might have been brought about by degrees, and nothing is clearer to me than its proving infinitely advantageous to Britain. It would have given an annual certain export to her; it would have rendered common husbandry so little profitable in North America, that the northern colonies, from whom we have so much to apprehend, would not probably have been one fourth so populous; instead of which we should have had many more people than we have to the south of Pensylvania, and consequently larger products of true staple commodities. It should not be forgotten, that one man employed upon tobacco, is of far more worth to Britain than forty New England farmers. It appears therefore sufficiently clear, that we may deter-

determine corn and provisions to be very improper commodities for a colony to deal in, and by no means to be ranked with staples.

Thus does it plainly appear, that a very strong distinction is always to be made between the colonies north of Maryland, and those to the south, in their importance to the mother-country; a distinction which should never be forgotten, as it will remain a lesson to all succeeding ages in what climates to plant colonies. The writer I before quoted, justly remarks on this subject—" That the staple productions of our colonies decrease in value, in proportion to their distance from the sun. In the West Indies, which are the hottest of all, they make to the amount of 8l. 12s. 1d. per head. In the southern continental ones to the amount of 5l. 10s. In the central ones to the amount of 9s. 6d.$\frac{1}{2}$ In the northern settlements to that of 2s. 6d. This scale surely suggests a most important lesson—to avoid colonizing in northern latitudes! Eighteen pounds the export of Nova Scotia after several years settlement, after the utmost attention from the government, after a million sterling of the public money being expended upon it, is an

exam-

example one would think sufficient to deter the boldest projector! But if our colonies to the north produce such trifling staples, those to the south, on the contrary, are immensely valuable;—indeed of such infinite importance to this nation, that *general expressions* of the benefit of our settlements should never be indulged; let provisoes ever come of—*those to the south*. We have found in the preceding enquiries, that those colonies which most abound with manufactures have the fewest staples; and this is a necessary consequence, for nothing but such products as bear a large price in Europe will yield a return from thence of the necessary manufactures, and much less of superfluous ones. But if a colony is situated in a climate which denies such productions, or from a want of due attention in the mother-country, they are not improved or suffered to decline, does it therefore follow that the inhabitants of such province are to go without cloaths, furniture, and tools? By no means; wherever there are people, they will most assuredly enjoy those necessaries; if they raise nothing from their soil which will purchase them in exchange, they will certainly
make

make them themselves. And if they are a populous flourishing people, they will find very little difficulty in the attempt. Indeed it is not, properly speaking, an *attempt*, but the regular course of things; a concatenation of causes and effects, which take place imperceptibly. And in proportion as they grow more and more populous, their manufactures will increase beyond the proportion of the people, until they come to work for exportation. It is ever to be remarked, that a people *cannot* FULLY supply themselves with any commodity without more than doing it—some exportation must take place, or the home consumption will not be regularly satisfied. It likewise appears, contrary to the ideas of several modern writers, that it is very possible for cultivation alone to supply a people with *all* the necessaries of life without any assistance from *trade* or *manufactures*; and that under the disadvantage of exporting the raw material, and importing the manufacture, by a long and expensive voyage, under the subjection of duties, and consequently under complicated charges. The inhabitants of the West India islands and the southern continental colonies wear not a rag a rag of their own manufacturing; drive not a nail of their own forging; eat not out of a platter or a cup of their own making; nay, the former produce not even bread to eat; and if that was the cafe with all the reft, provided Britain could regularly fupply the deficiency (which under a certain fyftem of policy fhe undoubtedly might), it would be fo much the better for her;—fo entirely do thefe colonies depend on the mother-country for all manufactures! and all from poffeffing beneficial ftaples. Of fuch vaft confequence is it to the country to plant new colonies, or extend our old ones, only in climates which will allow of fuch capital advantages."

In this enquiry I have endeavoured to fhew not only the importance of the American colonies to Britain, but at the fame time to explain wherein that importance confifts; we find it lies in the climate of the colony being different from that of the mother-country, as therein confifts the only probability of the people going upon ftaple commodities. The northern fettlements might be made of much more advantage than they are at prefent; but it would

would be anticipating the subject to consider that point here, as I shall in another essay endeavour more particularly to explain it.

CHAP. XXXV.

MANUFACTURES.

State of the colony manufactures—Difficulties under which they lie—Means of putting them down—Buy up the raw materials—Bounties—Finding other employments—New colonies—Observations.

MUCH has been written concerning the bad effects of the American colonists going into manufactures, but no satisfactory account has been given of the amount of such fabrics, which has been owing to Parliament's never having ordered a return of them to be laid before them. Some late writers have urged strongly the magnitude to which these manufactures have arisen, but it has been from calculations founded on dubious authority. In this case the general idea of the necessity of *making* that we cannot *buy* would be satisfactory, did we know the amount of their consumption, and that of their means of satisfying it.

In considering this point, we are to drop the idea explained in the preceding chapter, of the ill consequences to Britain which resulted from their trade and fisheries, and here merely take them as means of acquiring wealth, wherewith to purchase manufactures,

By manufactures are not to be understood the fabrics of private families, who work only for their own use, but those only that are wrought for sale, and which are the only or principal livelihood of the persons concerned and employed in them. This is a distinction which our writers have not attended to sufficiently; for tho' the population of a settlement that entirely supports itself is of little or no value to Britain, yet as it is passive, and no more than supports itself, it is much to be preferred to another branch of population, which is employed in cloathing, &c. itself and others too—that is, manufacturing for sale. As to the first evil, no remedy in the world can be applied to it that will be effectual; nor is it an object which can ever

ever claim the attention of the mother-country.

It is from hence clear, that the object of enquiry is not the probable total consumption of all the people in the colonies, but of those only who do not work up their own manufactures: when the northern settlements are compared with the southern ones—it is of consequence to shew the great superiority of the latter; but as that superiority was fully shewn in the last chapter, it is not to the purpose here. The only consumption to be considered is that of the ranks which *buy* in order to consume. Their making the purchase, shews that they have wherewith to pay; and then comes in properly the pretensions of the mother country, *if you buy, I expect you buy of me.*

Nothing is more difficult than to discover the amount of their manufactures for sale: we are to consider that there are other articles in their imports besides manufactures, wine, rum, sugar, India commodities, &c. all which amount to considerable sums. The means by which they can purchase those and manufactures are their exports, the produce of their lands—the produce of their fisheries, and the profits of their commerce; the two first are pretty well known, but the latter, open and clandestine, is very great, and no guess can be given of its amount.

That the manufactures for sale are not so great as some have imagined, may be conceived from the vast number of inhabitants, who in all probability work entirely for themselves; in a country where the minute division of landed property is so great as in the most populous of the northern colonies, and in a climate that will yield little valuable, it is impossible that the people should be able to *purchase* manufactures: poor countrymen in England do it because all their income is paid them in money, whatever may be their work; but in America day-labourers are rarely to be found, except in the neighbourhood of great towns; on the contrary, the man who in England would be a labourer, would there be a little freeholder, who probably raising for many years but little for sale, is forced to work up his wool in his family, his leather, and his flax, after which, the rest of his consumption is scarce worth mentioning. The number of people in the northern colonies who come under this denomination is very great,

great, and consequently the deductions to be made from the total consumption very considerable: it is not a difficult matter to calculate how much a head would supply the total of a people with manufactures; this has been calculated; but it is extremely difficult to guess the amount of *purchased* manufactures, which is the only important point.

In this enquiry we should not confine ourselves to the northern colonies, but take into the account that part of the population of the tobacco ones which is not employed on tobacco; a considerable proportion of the total: as any person may judge who recollects that soon after the peace the number of people in Virginia and Maryland was calculated at 800,000, the export of tobacco therefore is not much above 20s. a head; instead of which, those who are employed by that staple are able, in all probability, to consume 5, 6, or 8l. a head in imported commodities, and the rest of the people scarcely any thing, as they must, like their brethren to the north, manufacture almost every thing they use. If the imported commodities in these colonies are assigned to 200,000 people, there will remain 600,000, whose purchased consumption is small; and if the common calculation is taken, of their being at the peace 1,000,000 of people in the northern colonies, we then find 1,600,000 souls, among whom the imports are in some proportion or other to be divided. The exports from Great Baitain are as follow:

	£.
Canada,	105,000
Nova Scotia,	26,500
New England,	407,000
New York,	531,000
Pensylvania,	611,000
	1,680,500

If the population of these was 1,000,000, they imported about 32s. 6d. a head: if we allow 5l. a head for all that *purchased* their consumption, the number this importation supplied is 336,000, at which rate (to speak nothing of West Indian and foreign imports) 664,000 persons manufactured for themselves, besides the proportion of the tobacco settlements. Hence if these data are just, we may suppose one third of the people to consume purchased commodities, and two thirds to manufacture for themselves; but this supposes their own

own fabrics for sale to be inconsiderable, and that 5l. a head is for only a partial consumption.

There is yet another light in which this point is to be viewed, which is a different classing of the people; for the sake of explaining the clearer what I mean, I will suppose a division of the million of people in the northern colonies.

200,000 who consume of foreign manufactures, &c. only 2s. 6d. a head.
500,000 who consume a head 40s.
300,000 who consume 5l.

The first,	-	-	-	25,000
The second,	-	-	-	1,000,000
The third,	-	-	-	1,500,000
				2,525,000
Import from Britain,		-	-	1,680,500

According to this account, they must buy of foreigners, or work among themselves for sale, to the amount of } 844,500

For in this idea the fabrics worked in private families have no place; if they were taken in, the poorest would consume far more than 2s. 6d. There is nothing extravagant in this account; nor can it be supposed that the manufactures of the northern colonies amount to less than 844,500 l. In case the consumption of the classes here stated is greater, then this amount will of course be proportionably larger.

Supposing this sum to be the fact, or near it—or if we call their manufactures for sale a million, I do not think it an amount that ought greatly to alarm the mother-country, provided she took proper measures to obviate their ill effects, which measures would be very easily planned and executed. It is to be remembered, that a very considerable portion of this sum must be expended in fabrics, the whole of which Britain cannot expect to furnish—and which in fact she does not furnish to any colony, for the last hand, to a variety of articles, cannot be put at London, but must necessarily be executed in America, and the labours of those workmen and artizans is there blended with the price of the manufacture.

All that this kingdom can expect from the northern colonies, is to keep down public manufactories, which take the wool from the sheeps back, and convert it into cloth; the flax from the ground, and make it into linen and lace; the skin off the beast, and turn it to finished fabrics of leather; the iron from the ore, and convert it into the variety of utensils which

which Sheffield and Birmingham exhibit; and the same in other instances: but this reasoning must not be carried too far in any of these articles; there are objects which when completed from wool, leather, and iron, will still be of such small value, that the very freight from Britain and carriage to the consumer would be twice the worth, such we may be sure will be wrought in the colony. But when we see them making cloth of 12 s. a yard, linen of 5 s. hats of 16 s. each, locks, keys, and curious articles of hard-ware, which is the case, we may then be certain that the policy of this kingdom is deficient; and that without violence, such manufactures might be put down.

We are to remember, that the colonists are under great difficulties in their attempts to raise manufactories for sale. The mother-country has the power of introducing her own fabrics as cheap as she pleases, and under whatever advantages of bounties or premiums she likes to grant; which she can do in her exportation of them to no other market. Every where else they meet with duties on importation, and perhaps prohibitions; but in America the manufactories of Britain are openly in every market

market without duty or clog. In the next place the price of labour is very great, greater take the year through than in Britain, which is a material article; this muft neceffarily be the cafe where land can be had for nothing; workmen may be gained for high wages, but thofe high wages will prefently enable them to fet up for planters in a country where twenty pounds is a fortune fufficient to begin with; thus the mafter manufacturers can never keep the men after they have got them, which muft lay them under almoft infuperable difficulties; or fubject them to expences which will make their manufactures much dearer than thofe of Britain.

The long winters and fevere feafon which ftops moft employments, have been urged as reafons why they may manufacture largely for fale: but I am not of this opinion; thofe who are converfant in our fabrics well know, that in very fharp frofts many of our manufactures are at a ftand; what therefore would be at Bofton or New York, where the frofts are in common 20 degrees fharper than the moft fevere we feel in England; and where the whole winter is froft and fnow: people can fcarce keep their extremities from freezing who

who attend to nothing else, how therefore could the finer sorts of manufactures be carried on? What sort of work would a weaver make, whose fingers were numbed with cold; or a workman in steel, whose flesh froze to his manufacture? In such a climate manufactures must be carried on in mild or warm weather, and then the workmen may have what they will ask in the field, and all the advantages here stated are at once given up. Under such circumstances no fabrics can be made cheap enough to under-sell Britain, but such as come extravagantly dear from her, and can be made reasonable in America; or others so inferior in kind, that freight and carriage make a large proportion of the whole value.

But supposing the manufactures of these provinces, notwithstanding these inconveniences, did not get to any height, which in some articles is the case, then Britain might, without having recourse to what governor Pownal hints at, excises, take measures that would bring them down. The easiest and most adviseable way would be to raise the price of their raw materials, by buying it up for the British market: the obvious way to bring about any such transaction

action as that, is by giving bounties upon the import into Great Britain, and if they are large enough, they certainly will effect any thing. But the objection is, that, in order to create a new trade, the expence, by way of bounty, may be greater than if done by other methods: I would propose to force the import of wool from the colonies into Great Britain to such a point, as would be sufficient to burthen the woollen manufactures of America, by raising the price of their raw materials: at the same time that this laid a tax on the American fabrics, it would give a bounty on the British ones, by lowering the price of their raw materials by the import from the colonies.

The employment of factors, agents, or contractors would be less adviseable far than giving a bounty, provided the latter would have the effect; but as the wool-dealers in the colonies must be thrown into a different channel, and as the merchants there must open new correspondences, a bounty, in order to force such a new business, must probably be a greater expence than if government did the business, at least for a time, through the merchants; but when once the business was brought near

near a regular train, a small bounty would have a greater effect than a large one at first.

Such a transaction would be very heavy upon the manufactures of the Americans; for under the disadvantages which I before stated the colonists to lie, a rise of price in their wool would have the same effect as laying an excise upon their manufactures, but which would be brought about without the heartburnings and disputes inevitable with a new tax. The idea of importing wool from America is not a new one; Dr. Mitchel some years ago remarked—" The wool of the colonies is better than that of the English; it is of the same kind with the Spanish wool, or curled and frizzled like that, and might be rendered as fine by the same management. By the step which the colonies have lately taken to raise all the sheep they can, they will have plenty of wool. With this they have already made cloth worth 12 s. a yard, which is as good as any that is made of English wool. Some of their wool has been sent to England, where it sold for the price of the best. This may perhaps be looked upon as a loss to England; but if she would study to make a right and proper

per use of her colonies, this might be of more service to her than any one thing they are capable of producing. If the Spaniards succeed in their attempts to manufacture their wool, England may want it from the colonies more than any other commodity, as it is well known there is not a single piece of fine cloth made in England without Spanish wool." This observation came from a person perfectly well versed in American affairs from a long residence there, and shews how expedient the conduct would be, with a view to the goodness of the wool, as well as the design with which I propose it to be done.

The same conduct might be pursued with some other raw materials, such as skins, hemp, and flax, all which are valuable articles to be imported into Great Britain; some of them are so already, and if our demand was a little quickened, it would certainly be laying a difficulty upon the American manufacturers that work them. It is true, that in both these cases the price would rise upon ourselves as well as them, but this I do not apprehend would be of a bad consequence equal to the advantages on the other side of the question; since there is no object in the policy of Britain

tain which is of near such importance as putting down, or at least preventing all increase in the manufactures of the colonies.

There is another method of effecting this great purpose, which in some respects would answer better, though worse in others: it would be giving a bounty on the export of such British manufactures *to America* as the colonists have made the greatest progress in erecting—and this bounty should be sufficient to enable the merchant importer in America to under-sell the manufacturer there: this would be a very simple operation, and might be made perfectly effectual; but it would have this needless expence, it would supply the West Indies and the southern continental colonies with the same fabrics as cheap as the northern colonies, which, though an effect of no ill consequence in itself, would add to the expence without making an equal return for it: not however that it would be without any return, for those British goods being so much cheaper in those markets would extend the consumption of them, and certainly increase the trade in them which is carried on in the West Indies.

Whether

Whether this method or the firſt was choſen, would not be materiel, provided the thing was done: but that ſome method ſhould be taken to effect it cannot be doubted, ſince the grand intereſt of Britain in her colonies is defeated and perverted by their ſetting up manufactories for ſale, a ſtep which, in the natural courſe of it, if left to itſelf, muſt inevitably bring on their independence.

But here it will naturally be remarked, that to put down the manufactures of the colonies, and thereby throw people out of employment, would be a very iniquitous ſcheme, unleſs ſome proviſion was at the ſame time made in an increaſe of other employments; and certainly no perſon can diſpute the truth of this; but this part of the work would be very eaſy: among the true ſtaples of the northern colonies have been mentioned ſkins, drugs, ſhips, pitch, pot-aſh, timber, flax-ſeed, copper, and iron, all which articles, particularly timber, ſhips, pitch, and iron, may be had in any quantities, provided due encouragement was given to procure them. At the ſame time that meaſures were taken to leſſen their manufactures, we ought alſo to

increaſe

increase the quantity of these staples, not only to give employment to the people instead of manufacturing, but also to supply the country in general with as much or more wealth than they made by that employment. Among these articles none have oftener exercised the pens of ingenious men than that of naval stores, which we import from the Baltic at so large an expence, and pay for almost entirely with bullion: our northern settlements produce all sorts of timber in as great or greater perfection and plenty than the east country; this is a point acknowledged by all; masts, boltsprits, plank, deals of all kinds, and some articles of timber much more valuable than what we import. Great objections used formerly to be made, for want of saw-mills being erected; but that is no longer the case, for there are many of them now upon almost all the rivers of America; so that every thing is done that could facilitate the supply, was the article of freight got over. *Gee*, in his *Navigation of Great Britain considered*, says, " Our plantations in America abound with vast quantities of timber, and the navigation from New England, Nova Scotia, or Newfoundland, is not more tedious, nor at a greater

greater distance from us, than the bottom of the Bothnic gulph, or Petersburgh. But those places having been long in trade, and having a constant demand from us for that commodity, they always have great stocks of timber ready squared, and boards lying ready to load a ship of five or six hundred tons in ten or twelve days; but hitherto we have never had stocks lying ready in our plantations, nor any encouragement for building large bulky ships, such as are used by the Danes and Swedes, who sail with a few hands and at a small charge. What timber we have had hitherto come directly to England, has been rather put on board to fill up, when tobacco or other merchandize has not been to be had, and therefore no care has hitherto been taken to make it a regular trade." But this is not at present the case; for I am well informed that there are large stocks of timber lying in many of our plantations ready for the West Indies, and proportioned to that demand, consequently the quantity would of course increase, with any increase of demand, and no difficulties of that sort would be found. But Mr. Gee is mistaken in his assertion of the length of navigation; for this is seen in the freight:
that

that from Riga to England is not above 25s. calculated at the rate per load at which it is paid for; whereas the freight from Nova Scotia is 40s. to 50s. This difference will, I believe, generally be found; and another circumstance in favour of the Baltic, is the price of labour, which is not half what it is in our colonies; these are the only superiorities of the east country. But on the other hand, our American timber comes duty free, and even with a small bounty, though an insufficient one; the only object therefore to get over is the freight; and this can only be done by giving a bounty per ton on all ships belonging to Great Britain that bring timber or naval stores from the colonies. Let us suppose the freight per ton from the Baltic 1l. 5s. and that from Nova Scotia 3l. which we may venture to state as an average, though 2l. 10s. or even 2l. may be sometimes taken; in this case, a bounty of 2l. per ton would turn the scale of freight by 5s. which, with the duties on the Baltic timber, would at once change the course of all the timber and iron trade. By various accounts it has been found, that our import in iron is 27,500 tons at 12l. is 314,000l. and timber 200,000l. these two articles amount

amount therefore to more than half a million sterling, not to speak of increase in the other branches of their staples. I before shewed, that the manufactures for sale in the northern colonies probably amounted to more than 800,000 l. a year; now we find that in these two articles of iron and timber they might earn of Britain alone above 500,000 l. which would enable her to take proper measures to sink their manufactures to that amount, and at the same time leave them with as much wealth as they had before—no hardships would be found from it in the colonies, but the interest of this country would be prodigiously advanced; instead of paying half a million to the Baltic in cash, we should send to the same amount in manufactures to America, the difference of which is very great; and at the same time we should effectually prevent the increase of manufacturing in America, which in future would prove of much more consequence than can at first be imagined.

The expence to the public at which these beneficial effects might be brought about, would not be large. One hundred thousand pounds a year would pay the bounty on 50,000 tons of shipping, that is, 100 sail at 500 tons each. We may venture to assert, that this navigation would answer the purpose, if confined to that alone; and the expence of such a sum would bear no proportion to the immense advantages that must inevitably accrue from it to this country.

By the export of naval stores the colonies would find employment for that surplus of their population which has driven them to manufactures—by the import of British manufactures in consequence, and the buying up of their raw materials, their own fabrics would be put down—the manufacturing interest of Britain would be most highly advanced, and the export of bullion to the Baltic would be stopped; all these advantages would surely be well worth the sum they would cost the public in the bounties, which would not be lost to the nation or paid to foreigners, but distributed among her own people at home, to the invigoration of their industry. A late writer, after starting some proposals similar to this, remarks, " These sentiments are founded in reason, and tend to render Great Britain independent of the effects of that prodigious commercial manufacturing spirit, which is now arose in all Europe.

There are many peculiar motives for importing wool from these colonies with the other articles already specified. It would be a great assistance to our own woollen manufactures, and at the same time have the best effect we could wish upon that of the colonies. No *importations* are more beneficial than raw commodities, to be worked into manufactures; and no *exportations* so pernicious to a manufacturing country as that of such raw commodities; for which reason Britain should wish to import wool from these colonies; and were the system of policy I am now sketching thoroughly executed, such importation might very easily be effected. Every particular of this system is the link of a chain, and all equally connected; the more iron, timber, pot-ash, and madder were imported, the more likewise you might have of wool, for the more would the colony woollen manufacture suffer, and consequently the less would be their demand for that commodity, and then the additional demand from Britain, at a time when the British manufactures were poured into every market, would completely give her the command of all the American wool. This impor-

importation might be made to extend to a very large sum annually.

"As to ships, some may perhaps think the benefit resulting from them to the mother country more equivocal; but in a certain degree I should apprehend the supply from the colonies highly advantageous. In many cases it might be found advantageous to build men of war there. But leaving them out of the question, let us consider the repeated outcries and complaints that have been made in this kingdom for so many years, of the want of timber for ship building; and that such complaints are not ill grounded, every body agree. Now would it not be a very prudent measure, to reserve the timber in this island for the use of the navy alone, and depend on America for that for merchantmen? It is by no means advantageous to this country, whose agriculture is of such immense importance, to have any land occupied by wood that is good enough to yield corn, and consequently no more should be raised than is necessary; and supposing it necessary to raise all that is requisite for the royal navy, that is certainly the most; for there is no occasion to extend it to all that is used in merchant ships. The latter had better

better all be built in America. Nor would there be any necessity to lose the manufacturing of the hemp with which such ships were rigged, since we might import it raw from the new colonies, and re-export it to the northern colonies, manufactured into sail cloth with as little expence as much of the hemp lies under, now used by New England, &c. If Britain builds annually 40,000 tons of shipping (I am only stating a supposition), this at 3l. 10s. per ton would alone amount to 140,000l. a year. Nor can I see why the northern colonies should not build for all Europe. The building trade might easily be carried to the underselling all other countries, and especially when the culture of hemp and the working the iron mines are carried to perfection; for then there is no country in the world that will unite all the requisites for building cheap so completely as our colonies in North America; and that at the same time while all the benefit redounds to Britain alone, and without there being the least danger to her from such natural advantages in them. The danger would be great, if at the same time she suffered them to be traders and fishermen; but I laid it down as a rule to proceed upon, that

that trade, fishing, and manufacturing were put an entire stop to among them. Now the trade of ship-building has not only the advantage of selling timber (a mere drug in America) to great advantage, but of obliging those who bought it, at the same time to purchase some quantity of our hemp and iron. Thus if we built 100,000 tons of shipping annually for foreigners in our northern colonies, it would make up the former amount 500,000l. and I am very well persuaded that this might be easily effected. Supplying other nations with shipping cheaper than they have it at present, would be no objection to this plan, since all the benefits they would reap therefrom are not comparable to those which we should receive from taking their money. Nor do I think in true politics it would be the least adviseable to refuse French gold for men of war thus built: for we may lay it down as a maxim, that the French will never want as many or more men of war than they can man; experience shews this; so that our enemy will not meet us with a ship the more for our selling them. And most assuredly we had better take his money than let it be given either to the Swedes or the Genoese."

The

The reader will here observe, that this point of employing the northern colonists upon staples, or commodities which answer the same purpose, by way of enabling them to do without manufactures, would in the nature of things lower their fabrics, and take off all that eagerness for making a progress in them which has of late been so strong among the Americans. Give them employments more advantageous than manufacturing (which all that I have named would prove), and they will, in the nature of things, apply at once to them with as much avidity as ever they did to manufactures; for in the course of affairs in the colonies, it can only be the *surplus* of population that can found manufactories for sale.

And here it is necessary to observe, that this system of destroying the fabrics of the colonies by buying up their raw materials, giving a bounty on the export of the British manufactures, and employing the colonists on staples, might be vastly assisted by the measures before explained of planting new colonies in better climates: this would draw off yet greater numbers than the above mentioned employment on iron, timber, ships, &c. The population that is
to

to be commanded for manufactories can only be had when there is a surplus, which the lands do not take off. The northern settlements are very populous—the best lands taken up—new grants only to be had in spots which possess not the advantages which settlers necessarily are desirous of: when such difficulties increase, and at the same time the people vastly increased, it is the nature of things that the application to manufactures must increase proportionably; and the necessity of counteracting the ill effect every day must be more and more evident: that surplus of population arises merely for want of lands worth taking up, as the very term implies, for no such thing can be found while land is so plentiful as to yield an immediate and beneficial maintenance to every family that applies for it: hence it is that manufactories are established, and hence the propriety of finding new employments on staples for the people, instead of manufactures; the same principles act in pointing out the necessity of such new colonies. That every man without employment may meet with every possible inducement to settle as a planter rather than as a manufacturer: and while any such exist, we may be certain what choice

will

will be made; the country life in America has too much independency, too much plenty, and too many conveniencies not at all times to be embraced in preference to the business of manufacturing, which in every circumstance is so much inferior.

When land is difficult to be had, or not good, owing to the extension of the settlements, or to the monopolies of the country, the poor must be driven to other employments than those which depend on land; manufacturing, commerce, fisheries, &c. must then thrive in the natural course of things, unless some such measure as I have stated is put in practice in order to provide other employment. Such measures cannot be carried to the extent that is necessary with such an increasing people: the plan therefore to be adopted is certainly to prevent the future increase of the evil, by providing a motive for the fresh emigration of the people. Settling Canada, Nova Scotia, and Florida, is not providing any such motive, as it has long been found that the people of the other colonies will not go to them; but colonies on the Ohio, Mississippi, and in the Ilionois, would have this effect beyond any other measure in the world. The journey from New England,
New

New York, Jersey, Pensylvania, and Maryland is by means of the rivers in the back country, the Ohio, the Mississippi, and the lakes, as easy, cheap, and commodious, as can be wished: so that the people in those colonies who cannot get good land at home, may, at a very small expence, provide as much as they can desire in those territories, which are in every respect as excellent, in point of soil and climate, as can be wished. Water-carriage from the old colonies is absolutely necessary to such new ones as are designed to draw off the people from them. The inhabitants of America are so accustomed to do without expence, that they would consider a long land carriage of their effects as an insurmountable obstacle to their removal; I mean the lower ranks of the people, whose emigration the system of policy I have just been stating would most concern. But the passage to the tracts of country I have mentioned, is as commodious, especially by the Ohio, as they can wish, and would not fail to draw off a very great number of the people.

Here I have traced that system, the several parts of which could hardly fail of having the effects I have mentioned. -In the

the first place, buying up their wool and other raw materials would lay a tax on their master manufacturers, at the same time that it would be an advantage to those of Britain. Secondly, giving a bounty upon the import in America, of such British manufactures as the Americans had made the greatest progress in setting up, would enable us to under-sell them in all the towns in our colonies. Thirdly, buying up or giving a bounty on the tonnage of all ships that brought iron, timber, or naval stores from thence, would find employment for their people more beneficial than that of manufactures; which would not only prevent such people as are now employed on them from falling into distress, but would prevent others from engaging in them in future. Fourthly, planting new colonies in fertile and healthy countries would draw off that surplus of their population, which has hitherto thrown them into manufacturing; it would lessen their present numbers considerably, and be a drain to their future increase.

These several points of conduct aim at the same purpose;—a purpose too important to admit of any delay; which on the contrary requires spirited endeavours, and
such

such variations in the view as shall attack the evil on every side. One or two of these measures might do much good, but all of them are necessary, if a complete cure is intended; and prevention meant in future as well as present ease. Manufactures in these colonies have been owing to the increase of the people being beyond the proportion of fresh land to take off the surplus of population; nothing can either put them down or prevent their increase, but drawing off many of the inhabitants, by tempting them with a better country and plenty of land, and finding more profitable employments than manufacturing for such as stay at home. These are the grand objects: well pursued they would prove effectual in putting down all their manufactories for sale, and preventing new ones being erected; but if the work was not sufficiently executed thereby, the bounty on similar British fabrics would give the finishing stroke. The northern colonies under such a system of policy would no more have manufactures abounding among them of their own make, than the West Indies or the southern colonies, excepting what was the private work of families; an
object

object not of much jealousy to Britain, and even those would be much lessened by the same conduct. At the same time that this great and desirable effect took place, the manufacturing interest of the mother-country would be amazingly advanced more than by any other measure that could be devised; for the export to America would be increased proportionably to the quantity made by the American manufactories for sale, and the import of naval stores; so that instead of paying a vast sum in bullion to the Baltic for those commodities, they would be bought of the colonies with manufactures, a difference infinitely great. The trade and navigation of Britain would be greatly encouraged—and her American affairs would be thrown on a footing that would, if well pursued, be effectual in preventing those many evils which cannot but arise from the establishment of manufactures among the colonists. Such advantages are rarely to be gained without trouble or expence; but in this case both would be small in comparison with the benefit: the small bounties already in being shew that our legislature think the thing extremely desirable; but if they would ef-

fect

fect it, they must submit to a larger expence, in order to secure a profit of far more consideration than almost any expence.

CHAP. XXXVI.

INDEPENDANCY.

Great errors in the accounts given of the progress of population in America—Principles of increase — Dependancy connected with staples—Surplus of population— Power of the colonies—Observations.

THIS is one of the most curious and interesting disquisitions that can at any time demand the attention of this kingdom. The colonies we have planted in America have arisen to such a height of populousness, power, and wealth, that an idea of their future independancy starts into the mind of almost every man on the very mention of them in conversation: some assert the period near at hand, while others are willing to believe it yet at a distance; to enquire when it is to happen is not of importance; but to examine those circumstances

stances, whose tendency is either to accelerate or retard it, is an enquiry which is equally interesting and useful, since from thence may be deduced the plan of conduct which it is proper this nation should pursue, in order to secure a continuance of the advantages she at present enjoys, by means of her settlements in America.

Virginia, from its first plantation, has doubled its number of people every twenty years: this fact, which is well authenticated by actual enumerations, has led many of our writers into a most capital mistake concerning the progress of population in America: they have transferred it from Virginia to our colonies on the continent in general, than which a greater blunder could scarcely be made. Virginia is a settlement where the people are spread all over the country, quite to the mountains, among the hills, and even over them; and have been so for many years, owing to the uncommon inland navigation all the country enjoys; but in the colonies to the south the people are confined to the unhealthy coast for the sake of cultivating rice, the most unwholesome employment under the sun. Tobacco and wheat, which are the grand products of Virginia, will not

not grow in swamps and marshes; though the former requires a rich moist soil, yet it must be free from wet, and dry lands do for it, provided they are fertile; rich woodlands, for instance, where oak, hiccory, and locust trees are found: such lands in America are ever healthy; and as to wheat, it may be laid down as a maxim, that wherever it thrives the climate and soil are salubrious to the human body. Another circumstance is the climate of Virginia, which at some distance from the coast is as fine as any in America; it is the medium between the cold of the northern colonies, and the heat of the southern ones, as its situation is between both. Further, Virginia is without towns, the people make such advantage by their agriculture, that all are employed in it, consequently all are on the increase: they have neither merchants, manufacturers, nor fishermen among them.

If the reader considers these circumstances, he will find them extremely well adapted to increase the number of a people. The healthiness of the climate—the goodness, and at the same time dryness of the soil—the ease with which every man finds employment on the soil—the profit of agriculture exceeding that of any other profession. These are points which, when united with the plenty of land that most of our colonies enjoy, could not fail to occasion a very rapid increase of the people.

That this increase is not to be extended in idea to the rest of the colonies, will evidently appear from these circumstances in them being very different: in the north the climate is so very severe, that it is impossible population should thrive in the same degree as a more temperate one, for the necessaries of life must be had with more difficulty. In the southern colonies, the heat is too excessive, in the low country on the coast, where the planters confine themselves on account of rice, for the people to increase as they do in Virginia: in the northern colonies the soil is not comparable to what it is in the tobacco ones, consequently provisions cannot be had with equal ease. The same observation is applicable to the planted parts of the southern settlements, and will continue so till the back country is cultivated. In the northern colonies agriculture, is far from being attended with that profit which results from the culture of staple commodities; the consequence of which is, a large pro-

proportion of the people applying to other professions, which are far from having that tendency to increase, which is found in classes maintained by the soil: thus the people gather into towns, populous cities are met with, the bane of increase, trade, manufactures, and fisheries flourish: and although such may be thought to increase the people, it is a great mistake; those employments only find business for the surplus of agriculture; where is a town full of those professions, in the most healthy climate, that doubles its number from its own increase in twenty years? Yet is this done in Virginia: on the contrary, all great towns would be presently depopulated, if they were not supplied by the country. Another circumstance is the considerable tracts of country in the northern settlements that are fully peopled, and where land is as dear as in the cultivated parts of Great Britain. In such there cannot be that increase which is found in Virginia, where the people are spread so much more over the country.

It is here necessary to attend particularly to the progress of population in a newly planted country, in order to see from what principles the increase of the people arises, and what are the circumstances that draw them from the professions which depend on agriculture. The great increase found in Virginia has been owing to the plenty of good land in a climate that will allow of the culture of a staple. A man there who fixes upon a plantation, breeds his family of course to a knowledge of agriculture; the sons marry early, because they no sooner form a connection with the daughters of a neighbouring planter, than they think of marrying: it is the same in England, but what puts it aside is the difficulty of supporting a family; the young couple, as much as they may wish it, are obliged by prudence and their parents to wait till they can be settled advantageously, which often is till the chance of a numerous family is half cut off. In Virginia, and those parts of the other colonies circumstanced in the same manner, the connection is no sooner formed than the marriage ensues. The man takes up a grant of land, his father gives him a little stock, and assists him in building a house: money is wanting for but very few things, and a small sum all that is necessary; the business is then done, and the future success of the family undoubted. Such a state of the case not only brings

brings on marriages early, but also early courtships; for in thickly peopled countries men are retarded in their ideas of connecting themselves, for fear of that poverty they are always in danger of: an unmarried young man in parts of the colonies is a prodigy.

Here therefore we deduce the first principle, which is plenty of land to be had for asking, and under the payment only of some flight fees: the second is, that land being good, and well situated; if it is not good, too much expence and difficulty will attend the cultivation of it; for if subsistence for a family be not easily and speedily to be gained, with some surplus, by the sale of which other necessaries may be purchased; more money must be had in readiness before a plantation is undertaken, and if the situation is not within a due distance of water-carriage, it will be in vain to raise products for sale, as they cannot be sold.

From hence we find there must be a difference in the progress of the population of different provinces proportioned to these circumstances; the land in Virginia is much better than in the northern colonies, and it is in general far nearer to navigation; these are points of superiority which cannot

not fail of rendering the increase much quicker in the former than in the latter.

 The third observation to be made here is concerning the climate; the soil must not only be good, but the climate must be warm enough to yield products that are of a value sufficient to make agriculture more profitable than either manufactures, commerce, or fisheries. In Virginia the culture of tobacco is much more beneficial than any other employment; the crop yields a certain and ready value, by means of which they are able to purchase such manufactures and necessaries as their lands will not produce, and at the same time afford a good profit to the planter; so circumstanced they have no inducement to change their way of life—their sons have no other business before their eyes, by which they can better themselves even in idea. But all this is different in the northern colonies; agriculture there is nothing more than the culture of provisions, which, though when prices are high, and a market ready, is very profitable, yet is it not that regular profit which attends a staple; this want of a regular market for commodities rarely to be sent to Europe, renders other means of getting money necessary,
such

such as commerce, fishing, and manufactures; and when once these are but partly established, they must necessarily draw off many people from the culture of the earth. The success which attends some of these—and the inclinations of individuals, which, *when there is a choice*, will necessarily operate with many, by degrees lead more and more into pursuits entirely different from agriculture; circumstances owing originally almost entirely to a want of staple products. When once there is a population formed independent of agriculture, the people are divided; one part increase proportionably to the circumstances above described, but the other have no increase, or probably require the support of the country to keep up their numbers.

We find therefore that the first requisite is plenty of land in a healthy climate; the second, fertility and a convenient situation; and the third, the climate's yielding a staple product: if we examine the rest of the colonies with Virginia, we shall find them inferior to it. The plenty of land in the northern colonies is not comparable to that in Virginia, unless it be in places either not fertile, or in inconvenient situations; the navigation of Virginia is infinitely superior

perior to that of any other colony: New England has very little inland navigation; and in point of fertility, the soil in the tobacco provinces much exceeds that of any of the rest. Respecting the product of staples, the northern colonies have none, and therefore have been driven to every profession as well as agriculture. And in the southern ones, where there are both staples and good land, the rice culture has fixed the principal part of the people on the coast, where the climate is so unhealthy, that, instead of breeding people, it is formed for destroying them.

From these considerations it is very evident, that the increase of people in Virginia must be far greater than in the rest of the colonies, and consequently, that those writers who have supposed the whole of our settlements to increase in people as quick as that colony, must have erred very considerably in their calculations.

This is a material point: it is a very good thing for Britain, that the colonies which have not staples do not increase so quick, for if they did, their manufactures, &c. would increase proportionably; but that increase in other colonies brings on a corresponding increase of the staple products,

ducts, and also a proportionable consumption of British manufactures.

The independency of the colonies, whenever it may happen, must turn on this point, *the increase of people in those settlements which have not staples.* The increase in those which have staples, must always be for the advantage of the mother-country. It is therefore of consequence to know the truth of so important a matter: the northern colonies are most populous, but it does not therefore follow that their present increase is equal to that of Virginia.

Dr. Mitchel says, the number of people in the tobacco colonies soon after the peace was 800,000; in the northern colonies near 1,500,000; and in all the colonies 3,000,000; the total I do not apprehend at that time to be so great. The melancholy circumstance in this account, is the number in those settlements which produce no staples. If the total, as some authors assert, be 2,000,000 at the peace, the number in the northern colonies could not be above 1,000,000 or 1,100,000.

It is no difficult matter to explain how the danger of America's becoming independent does not lie in mere population,
but

but in the territories where that population is found. A people spread over a vast extent of fertile country, and employed in raising staples so valuable as to pay well for the freight to Europe and distant countries—the raising which is attended with more profit than any other employment—such a people, it is very evident, can find little or no inducement to oppose the designs of the mother-country. The latter finds a ready and certain market for all the staples of the former, and sells in return every article of manufacture or other commodities that can be wanted, at the same fair price she fixes on them in all other markets: at the same time that this friendly and mutually beneficial intercourse subsists between them, the mother-country is at all times ready and able to protect the colony against all enemies and invaders. In such a situation it is evident that both parties must remain satisfied with each other, until one of them is guilty of some great indiscretion or false politics; and we may venture to assert, that such false steps, in all probability, will come from the mother-country, that is, from the active and superior party, This is the true description of a colony founded upon just principles,

and

and the great object to be attended to is the people's employing themselves in a business wherein they cannot interfere with Britain.

Now if we turn our eyes to the northern colonies, we shall find that the case is extremely different. As the climate will not produce staples of value enough to purchase manufactures, &c. the inhabitants are necessitated to apply to other professions; these are commerce, fisheries, and manufactures; the moment they get into this train, they engage in a rivalship with the mother-country; both are in the same pursuits; they meet each other in the same markets, and with the same commodities; when once the mother-country *feels* the effect of such a competition, jealousies, heart-burnings, restraints, opposition, and a number of effects of rivalry arise, and are the fore-runners of that independency of which we are treating at present.

It is not that the northern colonies are without a considerable and a profitable agriculture; the distinguishing circumstance is the product of the agriculture. In the tobacco colonies, &c. the staple is a commodity that is wanted in Europe, and yields a good price, consequently the planters

planters can sell to the British merchants a product that regularly supplies them with a return of British manufactures. But the agriculture of the northern provinces, that is, of all the settlements north of the tobacco colonies yields only corn and provisions; valuable articles, it is true, but not sufficiently so to bear the freight to Europe, except in years when they are very cheap in America, and very dear in Europe: consequently the sale of them to the merchants of Britain must, in the nature of things, be a mere uncertainty, a contingency depending on accident: whereas the sale which is to pay for the import of manufactures must be regular, and absolutely to be depended upon.

Now the want of such staple products must have the consequence of obliging the inhabitants of such colonies to make those fabrics they cannot buy, or else to apply to such businesses as may have the effect which the agriculture of other colonies produces.

But, say some, why cannot these settlements apply to manufactures, commerce, and fisheries, without such an application bringing on their independency?—Because those employments, by whatever people they

they are carried on, occasion wealth, military power, and that surplus of population from which armies may, on any occasion be raised. When the general business of a colony is the same as that of the mother-country to the degree of rivalship, disputes and quarrels must arise; and when these become inflamed by a continuation of the same disputes, the possession of a great body of seamen, many ships, with every sort of naval stores, arms, and ammunition for the equipment of fleets, armies, and their attendants, with a great surplus of population for the recruit of both; manufactures in number sufficient to take off a dependence on others, and commerce for a general supply; when this is the case, it must surely be apparent, at first sight, that colonies in such a situation possess the principal means of becoming independent; in such a situation they will have little compunction at disputes with their superior, and every day feel less and less dread at any open hostilities.

The difference is extremely great between such and others that are in a different predicament; among whom we find no surplus of population, no ships, no seamen, no magazines of naval stores, nor any

any great cities, to plan, direct, and head the discontents that may arise from the causes I have just set forth. While the natural tendency of the soil, climate, productions, and navigation is to spread the people over a whole country, their increase does not make them powerful; add millions to Virginia, and spread over the Ohio, Ilionois, and Mississippi, they will be no more powerful with four millions than with one, because, as long as fresh land is plentiful, there will be no surplus of population to gather into towns; without the same surplus there can be no manufacture, nor any possibility of raising armies or navies. A colony not a fourth so populous, but possessing a surplus of population apparent in its cities, and consequent employments independent of agriculture, would be far more dangerous to Britain. Hence we find how ill judged a conduct that was in the British government, which lead it to attempt to force a capital in Virginia: every means were used to lead the people to flock into Williamsburg, and magnificent edifices erected to adorn it; miserable want of foresight! Instead of which, had great restrictions been laid on towns increasing, in the

infancy

infancy of Boston, New York, and Philadelphia, this country would at present have been in the possession of perhaps 20,000 seamen more than she now enjoys; and all the trade depending on them. A modern author observes, " The navigation than of our American colonies has been more once exerted in actual feats of power, in carrying on a war—against the enemies of Britain indeed; but the same power might be exerted against her, and in the case of a revolt most certainly would." " We have been here, says an American writer, but little more than one hundred years, and yet the force of our privateers in the late war (that of 1744) united was greater, both in men and guns, than that of the whole British navy in queen Elizabeth's reign." What therefore must it have been in the late war! Besides such a formidable naval force, they have raised, paid, and armed great armies. During the late war they kept an army of above 30,000 men on foot. They have founderies of cannon, magazines of war, arsenals, forts, and fortifications, and even victorious generals amongst their own troops. They have a standing militia; and constantly have the means of raising and arming a formidable body of forces. Let it not be imagined that I am drawing a comparison between the power of Britain and her colonies; far from it; I am only touching upon a few concurrent circumstances, which add to the grand ones of an independent agriculture and manufactures. Supposing that the latter are of capital importance to a people about to throw off the dominion of another, the former are likewise of vast consequence to the attempts, and would render the execution much easier than it could be without them: and how much likewise would depend on the situation of Britain at the time! For instance, whether she was in the midst of a succefsful or an unsuccefsful war;—in the midst of a secure peace or a doubtful contest. A certain concatenation of events might give the colonies an opportunity of not only striking the blow, but preventing all future hopes in the mother-country of reversing it. The effect of external circumstances therefore must be great."

Seeing the principles upon which the danger of this independency lies, we may, without great difficulty, examine and point out the means of preventing it as long as possible: we have found that the situation which

which most threatens it is the populousness of those colonies which have no staples: hence therefore all those measures I before pointed out as a remedy against the manufactures of America are equally applicable to the present case; since in their operation they cannot lessen the fabrics of the northern colonies without either lessening the number of their people, or in giving them employments which shall have the effect of staples. In proportion as these objects were effected, the greater would be the difficulty of their becoming independent; and in that chain of conduct no link is more important than the establishment of new colonies in such a climate as will yield staples, and in situations which will admit an easy emigration from the northern settlements to them. Such new colonies, among which that of the Ohio will be foremost, would have the effect of drawing off that surplus of population which in a country most of which is cultivated, applies to manufactures, commerce, or fisheries; and as long as such surplus could be made to flow in this new channel, we should be in no greater danger of the independency of America than we are at present, and perhaps not in so much.

I have shewn, that the general increase of people in the colonies is not near what the generality of writers make it: inftead of doubling all their numbers in 25 years, their prefent number will not probably be doubled in 50 years; and then the next doubling may take 120 years, and fo on; a confideration too much overlooked by all authors that have treated of American affairs. But granting the increafe to be quicker than I have ftated it, yet it is not the numbers, as I before obferved, but the furplus of agriculture that we are to fear.

Suppofe the total fifteen millions, but fpread over the continent fo much, that the manufactures, commerce, and fifheries were no greater than at prefent—in that cafe I affert, that we fhould be in no greater danger of their independence than we are at prefent. But on the contrary, if their numbers had filled all that part of the continent which will yield ftaples, fo that frefh land for a fmall expence could no longer be had for new fettlers, then of courfe that furplus of population which ufed to be taken off continually by new cultivation, muft necefarily have recourfe to other employments; then cities arife, commerce and manufactures flourifh, the arts are introduced, and a mother-country eftablifhed inftead of remaining a colony.

Here

Here we may make an observation, which, though at first sight it may appear greatly distant, yet deserves attention; whenever population has advanced to such a degree in our colonies: it is, that we must then, at all events, make the acquisition of Louisiana, on the west of the Mississippi, to supply that necessary quantity of fresh land which will be wanting to prevent the surplus of population applying to any other profession than agriculture: if the preceding principles are admitted, and they can hardly be rejected, then this observation will not have the appearance of wildness. The author above quoted gives an idea of British policy similar to this: he remarks, " That she should abide by the boundaries fixed already to the old colonies, that of the rivers' heads; and all further settling to be in *new colonies* wherever they were traced.—That she should keep the inland navigation of the continent, that is, of all the great lakes and navigable rivers to herself, and not suffer any sets of men to navigate them, and thereby communicate from one part of the continent to another.—That she should never suffer any provincial troops or militia to be raised, but reserve entirely to herself the defence of the frontiers.—That she should throw whatever obstacles she could upon all plans of communication from colony to colony, or conveniencies from place to place.—That in proportion as any colony declined in staples, and threatened not to be able to produce a sufficiency of them, the inhabitants should receive such encouragement to leave it, as more than to drain its natural increase, unless new staples were discovered for it.—A people, circumstanced as the North Americans would be, if such a system was fully and completely executed, could not possibly even *think* of withdrawing themselves from the dominion of Britain until their staples failed them, and they were drove, in spite of all laws and prohibitions, to herd together in towns for the purposes of manufacturing those necessaries which their staples would not pay for. No matter what their numbers might be, they would remain subject to the mother-country as long as she could supply them with staples, and that principally would depend upon providing their increase with fresh land. It is true she would find an end of her territory at last, and then the natural course of things would form towns and manufactures of that increase, which she before took off by means of plenty of land.

land. A connection would then arise between town and town and colony and colony; *numbers* would feel that strength which results from *connection* alone, and the influence of the mother-country would be too weak to oppose the consequences."

If a contrary conduct in Britain should be pursued, which it must be owned is but too likely, the independency of America may happen in no distant period; for as such progress has been made in the northern colonies towards general manufactures, and the possession of great fisheries and an extensive commerce, the effect will every day be an increase of those employments proportioned to the surplus of population in the settlements; and this increase must necessarily bring on a degree of power, which will enable them, on the first fair opportunity, to throw off their obedience to the British government. Or affairs may gradually go on in such a train, as will bring on he same independency by slow degrees, and at last rest in the completion of it without any acts of violence against Britain—by rising into too powerful a people for the mother-country to think of controuling.

X 4   CHAP.

CHAP. XXXVII.

REPRESENTATION.

Of a union between Great Britain and her colonies—Objections which have been made—Answers—Difficulties—Observations.

THAT different parts of the same empire ought to be united as closely as possible by all the ties of political interest, is a maxim, which as it has never been denied, so one might imagine it would never be necessary to prove the cases in which it ought particularly to be applied. But in this of our American colonies such difficulties have been started, and such objections have been made that have made many persons to think truth no longer truth—or that a strong exception is here found to a maxim otherwise infallible.

Mr. Pownal, who resided long in America, and was supposed to be well acquainted with American affairs, started the plan of an union in a more direct manner than any other writer of credit had done before, shewing that an American representation might

might take place without very great difficulties: and the late Mr. Grenville went pretty much into the same idea when he planned the stamp act, but from that blundering execution which was seen in all his schemes, he totally defeated the plan by beginning at the wrong end.

A very able and lively author, in the *Observations on a late State of the Nation*, took Mr. Grenville's scheme to pieces, and ridiculed it with great severity. His objections turn chiefly, if not entirely upon the distance of America, and the uncertainty of that navigation, from length of voyage, shipwrecks, and war, which must bring the American representatives to Great Britain: in all which he displays much wit and great ridicule. But I am one of those who do not think that wit is reason, or that he who gets the laugh must infallibly be on the right side; since this would be nothing more than saying, that a man's conduct is always right in proportion to the wit with which he can defend it. We are not therefore to see nothing but impossibilities in a matter which at most abounds with only difficulties; and a resolution to conquer difficulties ought always to be taken

in

in proportion to the benefits which will result from the victory.

The difficulty of the distance, I think, may be got over by several means, suppose the members from America, who may be there chosen either by the freeholders of the provinces, or by the present representatives in the provincial assemblies, should always be elected for an uncertain duration; that is, the member resident at London should continue the sitting member either till another landed who was to succeed him, or till his own re-election was noticed. I think this plan would at once answer many of the objections which the above mentioned ingenious gentleman has started. Nor do I see to what material ones the plan is open: if it is said that the member in England cannot support his interest in case of new elections in America, I reply, neither can the member of our own parliament, in case he is abroad, which often happens, and yet we see his friends exerting themselves near as effectually: but granting the fact, of what consequence is it to either Britain or America, whether Mr. George or Mr. Thomas be the member? As long as there must be a sitting one, the necessity

is

is fully anfwered by either; and if fome individual happens to be of fingular merit or popularity, he will of courfe be re-elected. This uncertain duration of a member's fitting may appear ftrange at firft fight, but upon a little reflection there will be found nothing objectable in it, as the term will be fixed by no minifterial artifice, nor by the artifice of any other man: if a member is not re-elected, it will of courfe be the bufinefs of his fucceffor to take his feat as foon as he can; and if on the way he fhould be taken by the Spaniards, and carried to Lima, it will be a difagreeable adventure to him, but public bufinefs will fuffer nothing by it.

But there is another circumftance which anfwers a great part of the objections which have been made to American reprefentation: Englifh counties elect Scotch members—Scotch towns elect Englifh members—and both of them Irifh ones; why not upon the fame principles elect Britifh members for America? They will be equally eligible. At prefent the provinces appoint agents, and give them falaries; why not elect the fame men into parliament; their feat will render a falary unneceffary, and they will be much more able to advance the

the business, and defend the interest of their constituents: it would be at the option of the electors of America either to chuse some person among themselves, or else upon the same principles as they make choice of their agents, to chuse some person of reputation or knowledge in Britain. There does not appear to be any insuperable objections to any part of such a business.

As to the arrangement of the electors in America, it would have no more difficulties in it than that of the same thing in Scotland:—it would only be necessary to take care that the increasing population of that vast country should be represented, which would be well enough secured by decreeing all freeholders, whose freeholds were above the value of ten pounds sterling—should have a vote, both such as were in being at the time of the union, and also such as should be gained or erected afterwards. And if the representation of towns was entirely dropped, it would be so much the better, and be taking a proper hint from the experience of electors in England.

Objections have likewise been raised upon the score of difficulties in contested elections, from the tediousness and expence of trials at the bar of the house, when witnesses

nesses are to be brought, and all their attendants, across the Atlantic ocean: but as well might we object to the representation of the Highlands of Scotland, because such evils were infinitely greater than with Middlesex:—there are boroughs in Scotland from whence it is near as difficult and expensive to get a tribe of people to London on such a business, as it would be from parts of America. If objections against extending legislation throughout the empire are stated merely from the extent of the empire, it is so weak a plea, that one might almost reply to it by saying, you should get rid of what you cannot govern. You can send governors, deputies, surveyors, marshals, registers, and placemen of every denomination to America; it is a pretty joke to imagine they cannot as well return us representatives.

Concerning the general expediency of this measure, I recollect nothing material that has been urged against it. On the contrary, very many reasons have been offered to shew that it is not only proper but necessary. It should be considered, that the danger of the American colonies throwing off what is commonly called the yoke of their mother-country, turns principally upon

upon points of government in which the one party is supposed to be aggrieved by the laws enacted in the other. Nor can we well state a case in which there is any probability of a revolt, but what arises from this circumstance.

If the union was to take place, and all the provinces of our American dominion represented in the British parliament, there would be a tye and a connection of a very different nature from what at present subsists between them. Acts of the legislature would then be acts to which themselves had given their consent; a point of vast importance, and by no means treated in a satisfactory manner, by speaking of a virtual representation.

Let us suppose the administration of our government to be so unexceptionable in regard to all American measures as to prevent any open revolt among that part of the subjects in our empire, in what manner then could America become independent? I reply, by the connection gradually falling off, until it became of no consequence—this connection is merely commercial. Its declension would be proportionate to the colonists supplying their own markets with manufactures, after which the remaining connec-

connection would be too inconsiderable to deserve a thought: hence therefore we find a natural and easy death to every advantage which can result from America to Britain. But if the former was represented in the parliament of Britain—and if that representation formed an entire new legislative power, to which they gave unrestrained obedience, the *connection* between them, which has been found of such importance, would be properly perpetual—as secure as the connection between Scotland and England.

If in any future time the population and importance of America become, what we have reason to suppose they will be, then it might be expected that a change in the place of parliamentary meetings might ensue, and America become the head of the empire, as far as the residence of government could make it so; a revolution which might be much more advantageous to this country than a total separation would be, under many circumstances which might attend so great a change. But as this idea is in reference only to a period extremely distant, no arguments to be drawn from it can be conclusive in the present enquiry.

INDEX.

INDEX.

A

AMERICA, sea coast marshy, i. 218—
ii. 47
Value per ton of the commodities of, 259
Population of, rightly managed, no cause of jealousy, ii. 93
Anguilla, climate, ii. 174
Farming in it, 175
Antigua, climate, ii. 163
Soil, 164
Produce, ibid.
Improvements, 165

B

Bahama Islands, climate, ii. 199
Healthiness, 200
Soil, 201
Improvements proposed, 202
Navigation, 204
Afford the most pleasing retreats, 205
Most agreeable and beautiful spots, 206

INDEX.

Barbadoes, climate, &c. ii. 151
    Soil, 152
    Progress of its culture, 152, 153
    Present state, 154, 156
    Profit from it to England, 155
    Proportion of export to soil, 157
    Culture of sugar in, 158
    Improvements proposed, 160, 162
Barbuda, climate, ii. 170
    Product and property, 171
    Farming there, 172
Bounties and premiums, advantages of, ii. 36
Buckwheat, culture of, i. 135
Buffaloes, ii. 88

C

Cabbages, culture of, i. 164
Canada, climate of, i. 16
    Soil, ibid.
    Husbandry, 20
    Exports, 25
    Importance, 27
    Defects in the agriculture, 31
    Compared with that of Great Britain, 37
    People in, 38
Cape Breton, i. 13
Carolina (North), climate, i. 330
    Products, 331
    Soil, 332
    Lawson's description of in 1700, 333
    Advantages of the planters, 337
    Cattle, ibid.

INDEX.

Carolina (North), husbandry, 339
    Fruit, 341
    Tobacco, 342
    Rice, ibid.
    Products of a plantation, 345
    Exports, 346
    Defects of their agriculture, 348
    Improvements proposed, 352, 358
    Advantages of the back country, 353
Carolina (South), climate, i. 367.
    Surprising degrees of heat and cold, 368
    Products, 376
    Timber, ibid.
    Fruit, 381
    Soil, 384, 387
    Back country, 388
    Rice, 391
    Indigo, 397, 400
    Expence and profit of a plantation, 407, 414
    Situation of the people, 432
    Exports in 1748, 434—in 1754, 440—in 1761, 441—in 1764, 443—in 1771, ibid.
    Improvements proposed, 446
    Madder, 467
    Hemp, 468
Carrots, culture of, in England, i. 210
Cattle, great stocks of, i. 167, 337
    Ill conduct of, i. 350
Ceded Islands, ii. 177
    Observations on, 196

INDEX.

Chartres (Fort), ii. 104.
Cherokee country purchased by Sir James Wright, ii. 33
    Fertility of, 34
    Propositions for improvement, 35
Christopher's (St.), climate and extent, ii. 165
    Soil and produce, 166
    Account of a plantation in it, ibid.
Codrington, (Christ.) account of, ii. 171
Colonies, importance of, ii. 208, 217
    Reasons for planting, 210
    Political management of, 213
    Regulation of commerce, 215
    Products of the British, 216
    Principles on which they should be planted, 222
    Number of people in, 299
    Manufactures of, 255
    Independency of, 289
    Power of, 305
Cotton, culture of, ii. 84.
Country gentlemen in England, state of, i. 68

D

Dominica, climate, ii. 177
    Soil and products, 178
    Sugar, 179

E

Egmont, earl of, his plantation in Florida, ii. 50
Emigrations, ii. 210

INDEX.

Export of corn from colonies, i. 88, 182
    Ill consequences of, ii. 246

F

Farming, profit of, in England, i. 202, 204
    Labour and teams to land in England, 311
Fences, i. 167
Fishery (Newfoundland), does not depend on planted settlements, ii. 245
Flax, culture of, i. 21, 55
    Native sort in Pensylvania, 162
Florida (East), history of the accounts that have been given of these countries, ii. 42
    Different accounts, 44
    New description, 45
    Climate, 46
    Soil and face of the country, 48
    Products, 50
    Plantations, ibid.
Florida (West), coast of, ii. 51
    Miserable country, 52
    Climate, 54
    History of settling, ibid.
    Political consequence of the Floridas, 57

G

Georgia, climate of, ii. 1, 6, 8, 9
    Soil, 2, 5, 10
    Back country, 3
    Productions, 4

INDEX.

Georgia, forests, 13
    Account of a plantation near Augusta, 14
    Great advantages of living in, 18
    Agriculture of, 20
    Cattle, 23
    Profit of agriculture, 25, 28
    Silk, 26
    Hemp, 27
    Planters in, 30
    Exports of, 32
Grant, Mr. his plantation in Florida, ii. 50
Greenville, Mr. George, his preposterous regulations, ii. 58
Grenada, climate and extent, ii. 182
    Character of, 184
    Products, 185, 187
    A plantation in, 188
    Errors in culture, 189
Grenadines, ii. 186

H

Hemp, culture of, in New England, i. 54 —in New York, 102—in Jersey, 137—in Pensylvania, 161—in Virginia, 257, 260
    Profit of, not equal to tobacco, 152
Horses, ill treatment of in colonies, i. 80
Hudson, river, account of a plantation on, i. 105, 108
    Great profit, 113
    Compared with husbandry in England, 116

INDEX.

I

Jamaica, ii. 111
    Climate, 112
    Hurricanes, 114
    Extent, ibid.
    Soil, 115
    Productions, 116, 143
    Sugar, 116
    Plantation in, 139
    Improvements proposed, 144
    A great improvement by Mr. K. 145
Jersey (New), climate, i. 132
    Soil, 134
    Defects in the husbandry of, 142, 146
    Timber, 141
    Fruit, 139
    Improvements recommended, 149
    Inhabitants, 152
Illionois, situation and description, ii. 99
    The finest country in the world, 100, 101
    Beautiful tracts, 102, 104
    Settlements near Fort Chartres, 105, 107
    Climate, 105, 106
    Products, 108
    Advantages which may be made of it, 109
Imports, British, from other countries, which might be had from the colonies, ii. 37, 38, 40
Independency of the colonies, ii. 289

INDEX.

On what turning, 299, 304.
Progress of, 301
Connection with agriculture, 302
Prevention of, 306, 310
Indigo, culture of, i. 397, 400
John, St. isle of, i. 13
Joseph river, St. country on, ii. 103

K

Kascasquias, French settlements there, ii. 107.

L

Labour, price of, i. 73, 169
Leeward Islands, ii. 163
Louisiana, Eastern, climate and extent, ii. 62, 64
    Soil, 66, 67
    Propriety of planting it, 68, 91, 93
    Forests beautiful, 70
    Timber, 70, 74
    Vines, 72
    Grapes and wine, 73
    Mulberries, 74
    Products, 75, 77
    Hemp, grows naturally, 76, 79
    Flax, 76
    Maize, 77
    Indigo, 78
    Tobacco, 79
    Of excellent quality, 80
    Silk, 82
    Cotton, 84

Olives,

INDEX.

Louisiana, Eastern, olives, 86
    Immense herds of cattle, 87
    Deer, 89
    Fruits, ibid.
    General advantages, 90
    Manner in which it ought to be settled, 94
Lucerne, i. 453

M

Madder, culture of in England, i. 211, 305
Maize, culture of, i. 77, 99, 134, 160
    Horse-hoeing, culture of, 51—ii. 76
Manufactures in the colonies, ii. 255, 257, 265
    Difficult to know the amount, 259
    Proportion to people, 262, 263
    For sale, 264
    Difficulties under which they labour, 265
    Means of reducing them, 267, 271, 276, 282
    To what owing, 287
Mississippi, navigation of, i. 292
    Its consequence, ii. 60
Mitchel's *Contest in America*, i. 286
Montserrat, ii. 169
    Produce, 170
Mortgages in England on American estates, i. 66
Mulberry trees in Pensylvania, i. 165
Myamis, French settlements on, ii. 107

Naval

INDEX.

N

Naval stores from the colonies, ii. 273
    Freight of, compared with Baltic, 275
Negroes, treatment of, ii. 138
Nevis, ii. 168
    Produce, 169
New England, climate, i. 45
    Soil, 46
    Settlements lately made, 48
    Husbandry, 50
    Timber, 56
    Exports, 59
    Inhabitants, 61
    Country gentlemen, 64
    Farmers, 66
    Their happy state, 68
    Errors in rural management, 74
    Compared to Great Britain, 86
    Gentlemen of small fortune much happier in New England, 91
    Tillage, 81
Northern colonies, peculiar circumstances of, ii. 235
    Great commerce of, 238, 240
    Ill consequences of, 241
    Illicit trade of, 243
Nova Scotia, soil and climate of, i. 1
    Husbandry, 4
    Characteristic of the country, 12

O

Ohio, climate of, i. 278

INDEX.

Ohio, settlement of, 279
    History of, 280
    Circumstances in favour of a colony there, 283
    Soil and products, 288
    Tobacco, 289
    Communication with the ocean, 291
    Hemp, 295
    Vines, 297
    Silk, 299
    Cotton, 301
    Indigo, 302
    Madder, 304
    Comparison with Britain in that culture, 308
    Expences and profit of a settlement there, 319
    Compared with husbandry in Britain, 327
    Junction of the Mississippi importance of that situation, ii. 69
Orchards, i. 103, 139
Orleans, New, strength of the Spaniards there, ii. 97, 98

P
Pens, confining cattle to, excellent husbandry, ii. 120
Pensylvania, climate of, i. 154
    Soil, 155
    Productions, 156
    Timber, ibid.
    Husbandry, 157

INDEX.

Pensylvania, labour in, 169
 Improvements proposed, 171
 Defects, 179
 Silk, ibid.
 Vines, 178
 Exports, 181
 Inhabitants, 184
 Method of living, 186
 Fruits, 187
 Plentiful living, 188
 Husbandry and living compared with that of England, 201
Philadelphia, price of land near, i. 174
 Society of agriculture there proposed, 180
Pine land, i. 384
Pitch, i. 342
Plantations, progress of settling them, and the expences and profit, i. 109
 First attention in settling one, 316
Poa angustifolia, in Canada, i. 22
Population of colonies, progress of, ii. 290
 On what depending, 292, 294, 296
Potatoes, culture of, i. 100—ii. 22, 173
 Great products in Barbuda, 173
Proclamation of Oct. 1763 condemned, ii. 63
Providence, isle of, imports from, ii. 200

R

Rain, the less there falls the more wholesome the country, ii. 46

Reeves,

INDEX.

Reeves, planter in Bay of Fundy, i. 6
Representation of the colonies, ii. 312
    Reply to the difficulties stated, 314
    Propriety of, 317
Rice, culture of, i. 342, 391
    Product and profit of planting, 395
    Dry, 463
Rice colonies, import of, ii. 224
Rolle, Mr. his plantation in Florida, ii. 50

S

Saffron, in New Jersey, i. 138
Scotch grass, ii. 133
Settlement, beginning of, and progress of a new one in Pensylvania, i. 190—in Georgia, ii. 15
    Account of one, 192—another, 198—another, 319
    Profit of, 325—another, 414, 424
Settling in America, advantages of, i. 116, 194, 245, 325, 427—ii. 16
    Compared with Britain, 197, 207, 213
Ships from colonies, of, ii. 279
Silk, i. 268, 354
Silk-grass, i. 274
Soils in America, signs to judge of, i. 313 —ii. 47
Sporting, perfection of fishing and shooting in Pensylvania, i. 186
Staples from Pensylvania, i. 183
    Importance of colonies producing, ii. 235, 253

Stores,

INDEX.

Stores in America, what, i. 227
Sugar, culture of, ii. 116, 118, 125
    Description, 116
    Soil for, 117
    Manuring for, 119
    Holing, 121,
    Weeding, 122
    Boiling, 124
    Rum, 125
    Buildings, 126
    Errors in culture, 127
    Improvements proposed, 129, 130, 131
    Objections answered, 132, 135
    Negroes, 138
    Expences and product of a plantation, 139
    Profit, 141
    To absentees, 167
    Culture in Barbadoes, 158
    ———— St. Christopher's, 166
Swamps, i. 387

T.

Tar, i. 343
Taylor, Mr. his plantation in Florida, ii. 50
Tobacco, culture of, i. 222, 246, 247
    Sorts, 225
    Inspection law, ibid.
    Product of, 227
    Profit, 229
    Necessity of fresh land, 230
    Nature of a tobacco plantation, 231

INDEX.

Tabacco, improvements recommended, 231
    Expence of culture an acre, 233
    Expences, and profit of settling a plantation of, 235
    Why the planters are not rich, 237
    Life of the planters, 242
    Superiority of the lands on Mississippi for, ii. 80
    Importance of, 227
Tobago, climate, &c. ii. 190
    Spices, 191, 192, 193
    Soil and timber, 191
    Products, 192

V

Vincent, St. climate, ii. 179
    Soil and products, 180
    Inhabitants, 181
Virginia and Maryland, climate of, i. 216
    Soil, 217
    Products, 218
    Timber, 219,
    Animals, 220
    Face of the country, 221
    Tobacco, 222
    Advantages of settling in, 243
    Comparison between a Virginia planter and a British farmer, 250, 251
    Exports, 256
    Hemp in, 257
    Husbandry of, 263
    Improvements proposed, 267, 272

INDEX.

Virginia and Maryland, silk, 268
    Vines, 270
    Hemp, 274

W

Waste lands in Great Britain, 249
    Not to be settled, 250
    Advantages of landlords farming them, 252
    Proposal to the legislature for settling, 254
Watering meadows, i. 166
Water-melons, i. 140, 102
West Indies, peculiar importance of, ii. 220
    Supply of, with corn, 240
Wheat, culture of in New York, i. 98
    New Jersey, 136
    Pensylvania, 157
    An universal grower, 182
Wine, from the colonies, i. 463
Wool in Pensylvania, i. 167
    From the colonies, ii. 269

Y

York (New), climate, i. 94
    Soil, 95
    Proposals for improving the husbandry of, 126
    Vines, 129
    Timber, 101
    Culture of grain, 98

FINIS.

www.ingramcontent.com/pod-product-compliance
Lightning Source LLC
Chambersburg PA
CBHW030008240426
43672CB00007B/865